UNVEILED SHADOWS
THE WITNESS OF A CHILD

A MEMOIR
BY
INGRID KISLIUK

NANOMIR PRESS
NEWTON, MASSACHUSETTS

ISBN: 0-9663440-0-6

Published by Nanomir Press, 1998

Newton, Massachusetts, Unites States of America

Inquiries should be addressed to:

Nanomir Press, P. O. Box 600577, Newton, MA 02460-0005
Fax: (617) 332-4770

Library of Congress Catalog Number: 98-91293
Kisliuk, Ingrid
Unveiled Shadows
The Witness Of A Child
Printed in the United States Of America
Second Printing

Production & Design: Robert B. Smyth

Logo By: Viviana Levinson

To The Memory of my Beloved Parents

Contents

ACKNOWLEDGMENTS

This book would never have been written without the constant support, encouragement, and help of Roy, my husband. I thank him with all my heart for his dedication and love, his belief in my work, and for his frequent proofreading. My gratitude goes to my daughter Michelle at whose urging I attended The First International Gathering of Hidden Children during World War II in New York where the idea for writing this book was conceived. I give her my profound thanks for her expert advice, for her encouragement, and for editing the manuscript and offering perceptive commentary. My thanks go also to my daughter Claudette for her proofreading and suggestions. I also thank my cousin Bette Joy Field for proofreading a large part of the manuscript, and my cousin Alice Terril for lending me family photographs. I am most grateful to my friends Myriam and Jean-Paul Cappelle, whom I had the good fortune to meet at the Brussels conference. They welcomed my husband and me to their home and kept in constant contact with us during our stay in Belgium. At the conference Myriam accepted, on her mother's behalf, a Righteous Gentile medal, awarded posthumously to her mother by the Yad Vashem museum in Jerusalem for harboring two Jewish children during the German occupation and for treating them as her own. My heartfelt thanks to Myriam, who helped my search for information in Brussels and later sent to me in the United States the full documentation of the assembly camp at the Caserne Dossin in Malines, the Breendonk concentration camp, as well as other important information. Many thanks also to Daniel Dratwa, curator of the *Musée Juif de Belgique* in Brussels for his guidance in my search for documentation. My appreciation to E. Reichert of the *Institut du Judaïsme, Institut Martin Buber,* at the *Université Libre de Bruxelles* campus in Brussels, for his help in locating useful books. My deepest gratitude to my friend Dorothea Mautner for her help in deciphering my sister's faded letters and postcards in German, which she had thrown out of the train en route to Auschwitz. Dorothea not only copied them by hand, but also lent me moral support during this painful task. My heartfelt thanks go to my friend George Brawerman for the many hours he spent with me working on his computer in scanning and printing the pictures, documents, letters, and postcards featured herein. I thank my friends Ina Friedman, Sam Starobin, Maria Orlowski, Robert Cowden, and Susan Suleiman for their good advice. I thank my friends Spencer Blakeslee, Joyce Antler, Jim Ross, Helen Fein and all the other members of my Holocaust study group. I also thank Régine Barshak, Diane McKirby, and Sol Gittleman for their encouragement and interest. I am grateful to Carolyn Ingalls, my copy editor, and to Robert B. Smyth, for their perception and skill. My heartfelt thanks to my niece, Viviana Levinson, for her artisitic insight in the drawing of the logo. And finally, my deep appreciation goes to Claudette and Michelle, my daughters, for their contribution in the "Afterword" of this book.

PREFACE

In Jewish tradition the unveiling of a tombstone takes place one year after a person's death. The members of my family who perished in the Holocaust have no burial grounds; they were laid to rest in this book. The letters and postcards featured here, which were thrown out of the train en route to Auschwitz - the names of these relatives now inscribed in memorials - bring closure to their fate. The unveiling of their graves took nearly half a century.

The following writing resulted from a moral imperative engendered by my experience attending The First International Gathering of Children Hidden During World War II [1] on Memorial Day weekend, May 26 through 27, 1991. Sixteen hundred people who came from all over the world, met in New York City. We listened to speeches in plenary sessions, and met in small workshops to discuss topics related to our past. There we discovered the many feelings we shared. Most of the participants had been reluctant to attend, fearful of dealing with painful memories. Yet, moved by a certain need, we came nevertheless. During these two days of intense dialogue and emotional exchange, a particular bond was established among the conference participants. The power of this collective bond and the sense of responsibility underlined by this gathering led me to decide to tell the story of my own childhood and thereby document, through my experiences, the events that occurred during World War II.

This book presents the personal account of an adult unveiling the experiences of a child. The process of writing was difficult; it was painful to uncover old hurtful memories that had been lying suppressed for many years, hidden in the crevasses of my consciousness. The rendering of an ongoing inner dialogue in the following pages resulted from my initial anxiety and questioning of myself as to the wisdom in attending the conference. This inner examination which continued throughout the writing, was a tool that enabled me to rekindle buried recollections and to face emotionally difficult memories.

The occurrences described, relating the experiences of my childhood from 1938 to 1945, are conveyed entirely from memory. As indicated, some recollections were recovered during the writing. I also point out thoughts and considerations which I had never contemplated before, that were brought to my awareness during the composition of the manuscript.

The documents, written records, and books that I discovered upon my return to Belgium, made the experiences of the past even more vivid and enabled me to document the events described in this book.

INTRODUCTION

Why would you go to a conference concerning a past that you have obliterated for decades and unearth such distressful recollections?

I kept questioning myself as I arrived and saw the former "hidden children," now mostly past middle age, having come from all over the world to connect with their painful memories. Almost all of them came reluctantly; they said that they did not want to remember, but they came just as I did, not really knowing why. About sixteen hundred people asked themselves: "Why now after nearly fifty years?" Yet not everyone looked grim; many people smiled and chatted animatedly. I wondered, why this attitude at the start of an event so disturbing to them?

Indeed, anticipating the release of so many painful memories, I was initially bewildered by the positive demeanor of many of the participants. Many had met previously and smiled greetings to one another. Others, especially people from abroad who had arrived the night before and had already gotten acquainted, engaged in spirited conversation. Why, then, did so many former "hidden children" come here, even if reluctantly? In retrospect, I believe that many came to bear witness to their ignored past, to admit openly the pain and desperation endured as children, and to acknowledge the consequences as adults. At last they affirmed, voiced, and expressed recognition of their tormented childhoods. Subconsciously they also searched for solidarity and strength by speaking of their mute past and by hearing others recall experiences that had been heretofore suppressed and often, for reasons of self-preservation, thought not to be worth discussing. For decades they had considered their lost childhood miseries insignificant; after all, who were they to speak of pain? They had been lucky, had they not, to remain hidden, not to be caught and deported to concentration camps? But now, collectively for the first time, they professed that what they have to say is especially pertinent, for they, the "hidden children," are the last survivors of the Holocaust. At a luncheon the keynote speaker touched a major chord when she noted that ours is the last generation to speak. As we age, if we remain silent much longer, the last witnesses will miss the chance to testify, to tell our own stories.

That speech had a lasting effect on me. Yet the consequences were not immediate, I wanted to disregard the uneasiness, the calling to witness that I experienced then. Still, the speakers words kept nagging at me until I finally recognized a primary goal for myself. I decided that although the pain of remembering may be overwhelming, the past must be documented. I had to recall experiences I have sought to forget, and to speak of them as others already have spoken of theirs, and as more will speak in the future. I needed to reconnect with my lost childhood, for the truth of history and for the memory of loved ones murdered in concentration camps. I also had to raise my voice to counteract the "falsifiers," the "deniers," the "revisionists" who try to obliterate the truth.

Still, how could I be sure that I could faithfully relate this distant past? Could I honestly say that I recall these events? Would I have the courage to dig deep down, to search? I had evaded finding my lost loved ones' names in the lists that Serge Klarsfeld[2] compiled in a book and brought to the conference. It was too painful, I avoided looking in his book for details of their deportation; I could not bear finding the transport numbers and dates on which they were shipped to the death camps from the assembly camp in Malines.[3] Yes, I evaded the torment - I knew their fate already. What use was there in knowing these details? They were irrelevant. At that point, writing was not a prospect. Later I decided to defy the anguish, to search for available facts, and for my own suppressed memories.

All along, certain doubts persisted. How could I finally speak about those years when I had concealed my identity in hiding as a child? With the imperative of survival, I had prevailed in erasing the past so well, to the point that I could not even be certain of the name of that Catholic convent, nor of its school that I had attended, which was run and administered by nuns. Yet all the while an inner voice kept urging me on not to find excuses. Finding the name of the convent and the school that sheltered me was simple enough: I would return to Brussels and find it. As for recollecting events, I could recall outstanding episodes, memories illuminated by their impact, by the anguish that they engendered, the fear and terror that they provoked and therefore were never forgotten. I would also check the dreaded "box," the metal filing box my parents had left me. As yet I haven't had the courage to look at its contents. I know that it holds many disturbing documents, among others the letter that my sister wrote from the assembly camp in Malines before she was shipped out to Auschwitz, the letters that she threw out of the rolling train, and the postcard that she sent from Auschwitz. In time I will find the emotional strength to investigate these valuable papers that bear witness to the past.

CHAPTER I
FLIGHT

I remember experiencing those initial pangs of anxiety at age eight in Vienna, the capital of Austria, where I was born. I heard the adults around me speaking of impending doom. They said that the Austrian Nazis had come out from underground where they had been waiting for Hitler to take over the country. Now with the "Anschluss," they were in power and we were all threatened.

I could no longer go to my excellent Jewish school, which was forced to close its doors. It had opened just two years earlier and I had completed first and second grade there, since my parents had enrolled me at its inauguration. I had been proud and happy attending that school. Although the school was secular, the curricula included Hebrew language and Bible study. We celebrated the festivals with song and dance. Chanukah was one favorite because it entailed wonderful presentations of the children's talent that the faculty sought to bring out in the students. My first experiences on stage date from that time. The school also sponsored an excellent summer overnight camp. I had participated in that camp for two weeks after the completion of the second grade. Although I spent the first week crying, plagued by homesickness, I recovered in the second week and especially enjoyed participating in the talent presentation at the close of the session.

Classes were held from Sunday through Friday, with Saturdays off. The school was staffed by lay administrators and faculty. Often, on my way to school on Sundays, accompanied by my big sister or by one of my parents, people we met in our building would question us and wonder about my going to school on a Sunday. Full of pride, I explained that I attended a Jewish school, and that our day of rest was on Saturday, the Jewish Sabbath.

Since all Jewish students were by that time barred from public schools, my sister Herta who was nearly seventeen, was not allowed to return to her high school, nor could my brother Ernst, who was nineteen, continue to study at the "Bauschule," a professional architectural school. The adults around me discussed how Jewish property was being confiscated and how leaders of the Jewish community, as well as other prominent Jewish citizens, were being arrested, jailed and deported. It was then that I heard for the first time the dreaded name "Dachau." In the windows of the small Jewish shops that had not yet been seized in my neighborhood, I saw big, ugly signs screaming the word "Jude." At the doors stood brown-uniformed *Sturmabteilung* (SA) sentinels, with wide swastika armbands, their bayonets held horizontally, to prevent gentile customers from entering.

The first incident that I experienced was when I was with my aunt Regin. My mother, Helene, had four siblings: one brother and three sisters. She was the next-to-youngest, and Regin was the oldest. Both had "Aryan" features and coloring. They resembled their own late mother, who also had had very light brown hair and blue eyes. The other three siblings resembled their father, whose hair and eyes were dark. Regin had just come to Vienna to attend my grandfather's funeral. She lived in Munich with her second husband, who was German and not Jewish. I was with her when she attempted to enter a small Jewish grocery store. The Nazi sentinel at the door barred our entrance with his bayonet. Regin insisted that she was indeed Jewish, but he demanded proof. She had no identification with her - her Aryan appearance gave her a lot of self-assurance - but she told me later that

The Kohn Family. Standing from left to right are the author's mother Helene, Regin, Grandfather, Eduard, and Pepi. Seated are Franzi and Grandmother

she had shown the guard a postcard she happened to have in her purse. Although it didn't identify her as a Jew, he accepted it and stepped aside. I remember that he looked amused. He probably didn't believe her and may have been entertained by the fact that she would pretend to be Jewish.

From our apartment windows on Tabor Strasse, in Leopoldstadt, a district inhabited by a large Jewish population, I saw many spectacles that frightened me. Standing next to my moaning mother, my being anguished increased by her lament, I saw young Jews being assaulted. They were outnumbered by Nazi thugs, and were unable and afraid to defend themselves. We watched old, religious bearded Jews dressed in black caftans being humiliated and beaten by young hoodlums while the policemen just stood by. Every day, long parades of brown-shirted members of the *Sturmabteilung* (SA) and *Schutz-Staffel* (SS) in their frightful black uniforms, as well as Hitler Youth, passed under our windows. With horror I heard the words of their marching songs emphasized by the pounding of their boots on the pavement.

"*Ja wenn das Judenblut vom Messer sprizt kommt eine bessere Zeit.*" (Yes, when Jewish blood spurts from the knife, better times are coming.)

The images evoked by these words filled me with dread and dismay. Why would these people want to knife me, my family, my friends? Why would Jewish blood squirting from their knives bring them better times? It was just a song - they could not possibly mean what they were singing! Alas, as further events would show, they meant it all too well.

Apprehension plagued me at the sight of the giant black swastikas on the huge flags that covered nearly whole facades of buildings, including well-known Jewish department stores, now "Aryanized." One of them, a clothing store named Schiffman, stood diagonally across the street from our apartment building. As I listened to the adult members of my family and their friends debate the current situation in hushed and anxious voices, I understood why we were isolated from all the excitement of the crowds in the streets. At last I comprehended the reason for the lavish decoration of the city! I had not known why all the lampposts were covered with evergreen, why garlands of greenery and flowers spanned our street. Now I knew that Hitler was expected to enter Vienna and that our street was on the itinerary of his motorcade. I heard many foreboding discussions of the news that all building superintendents had to furnish to the authorities a list of Jews living in the buildings they supervised. Jewish apartments with windows looking out on main thoroughfares were to be invaded by "Aryans" eager to view the motorcade. My parents had a good opinion of our superintendent and so expected him to manage the situation as best he could. They repeated his words spoken in Viennese dialect, that he had said to the inquirers, *"Ich habe keine denen Korkzieher von den Schläfen runterhängen."* (I have none who have corkscrews hanging from their temples.) Of course he referred to religious Jews who had come mostly from Poland and who still dressed in their traditional long black caftans. The "corkscrews" referred to were *"pe'ot,"* the traditional sidelocks. Many Austrian Jews still lived under the illusion, as did some gentiles, including our superintendent, that being assimilated and blending with the gentile population would spare us from persecution. Those fantasies would be quickly dispelled by the events that followed.

On the day of Hitler's arrival, people of all ages who were in a frenzy of anticipation, entered our apartment. Among them were a girl and two boys age nine or ten. The superintendent, who had succeeded in controlling the throng, led four people to each of our four windows overlooking the street. With excitement they awaited their hero and his entourage, and screamed *"Sieg Heil."* Perched on stools behind them, we could see over the heads of our "guests" the masses lining both sides of the street. When the motorcade appeared with Hitler standing in a convertible, his arm raised in his Nazi salute, the masses went into a frenzy, shouting *"Heil Hitler, Sieg Heil."* The street below was a sea of arms outstretched in Nazi greeting, and the noise of the cheering was deafening. The people at our windows shouted with wild abandon, *"Sieg Heil, Sieg Heil."* Once the motorcade had passed, they left chatting excitedly without a word or a glance at us.

The etching of those sights in my mind, the uproar and confusion, and the emotion and fear that it all engendered, remain indelible. Indeed, the view of the street overflowing with people screaming their approval and devotion to this man Hitler, was at once terrifying and riveting. Historical documents reveal that he was hailed by three hundred thousand enthusiasts on the Heldenplatz,[4] where his motorcade ended up and where he addressed the throng. The sight from our windows, as we stood on chairs and peeked down behind our "guests" to Tabor Strasse, offered a similar scene; the crowd was enormous. I have always remembered the sight and sound of that frenetic, screaming horde. This episode constitutes the beginning of my hostility. Of course, my total enmity for this population resulted from the accumulation of further horrid events that I was to experience.

Shortly after the arrival of Hitler in Vienna, my mother's father, who was seventy-eight years old and who had been healthy until then, became ill and died. Both my mother and my aunt blamed his death on the political developments as well as on his physician. They claimed that he had not received proper care. I was very sad, of course, but I was not as affected by his death as were my much older siblings, who knew him better. They had closer rapport with him and had helped nurse him during his illness. My grandfather's relationship with his younger grandchildren, my cousin Sonia who was three years my senior and myself, had been peripheral. I suppose my being the eighth in a row of grandchildren (my aunt Regin's eldest son Kurt having arrived seventeen years prior to my birth) made my birth no novelty. I cannot recall any memorable conversations with my grandfather. A large part of my sorrow at his death was due to the unhappiness around me.

Yet some evenings when the adults went out, my grandfather stayed with me and my cousin Fredi. At the time he was called by that diminutive. When he was older he became Fredl to the family, but I called him Fred. The incident in question occurred before the political trouble came to a head. I recall one episode when my grandfather, whom we called Opapa, stayed with us. As usual my talks with him were commonplace, about ordinary subjects. I often imitated my cousin, who tried to convince my grandfather to give him a few *Groschen* (smallest units of Austrian change). That evening Opapa fell asleep before we did, leaving us on our own. Doing this was not prudent on his part, for he must have known his grandson's knack for mischief. Twelve-year-old Fred, five years my senior, tried to convince me to use a very large lamp shade as a parachute and to jump out the window from our fourth- floor apartment. Luckily, I was not very intrepid and suggested that he jump first to show me the procedure. He thought better of the idea and instead managed to climb on top of a very tall armoire and to jump onto a couch as he held the lamp shade over his head. For Fred, jumping out windows from the ground floor apartment where he lived with his mother and Opapa, was a daily experience. He also loved climbing trees and jumping from the highest limb. Once he fell and broke his nose. It was somewhat flattened after that event so that he had a boxer's appearance. In any case, my mother never asked Opapa to babysit again after she heard that he had been asleep when Fred had suggested that I try parachuting.

Many years after the war when my parents and I had joined my brother Ernst in Argentina for several months, we recalled and lamented our loved ones who had perished in the Holocaust. Ernst reminisced about how Fred never left the apartment through the door, but always through the window, how he climbed trees, and eventually fell on his nose. My brother also recalled the times when Fred, who was seven years younger than he, summoned him to come to his defense when Fred was fighting with other boys and losing. My cousin lacked strong guidance in his home life. His father had died when he was an infant, and his mother found it hard to discipline him. In school his last mark in conduct had been a "4." (The grading system went from "1" to "4," with "1" being the best.) Receiving a "4" was considered a scandal in middle-class society. My sister Herta's school certificates almost always displayed "1" in every subject; she dreamed of becoming a teacher. Ernst was considered brilliant; he planned to become an architect.

In the first grade I obtained a "1" in every category of study, including conduct; in the second grade there were a few "2." No, I won't go to "the box" now to find my certificates and Herta's in order to verify them. My parents had saved the certificates through the years, and I had seen them many times. I know I keep avoiding examining the papers in that box, although I will have to eventually . . . , but not yet.

Opapa lived with my widowed Aunt Pepi and young Fred in order to give the boy a male authority in his life, and to a certain extent to assume the task of disciplinarian. Unfortunately, he was totally unsuited for that role and so was absolutely ineffective. Also, my aunt was the stereotypical dependent homemaker, since it was then unusual for women to have professions and be independent. Thus, being without a husband meant lacking financial support for herself and her son, but there my grandfather did manage to pro-

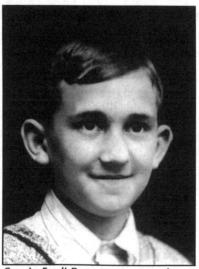

Cousin Fredi Dermer, at approximately age twelve.

vide adequately.

My mother and Aunt Pepi occasionally accompanied my father on his travels as a representative for Singer sewing machines. They assisted him in persuading customers to purchase the product. Since they could be very convincing, they were successful and loved the work. Also, anti-Semitism was rampant in Austria, and my mother's gentile appearance diffused some of the hostility that my father met in his business dealings. She would call on certain customers whom my father had found antagonistic and persuade them to close a deal. My aunt, even though her hair and eyes were dark, had no stereotypical ethnic features, so that she also could pass for gentile, especially when accompanied by my mother and identified as her sister.

The summer following the completion of my second school year and my first experience of summer camp, my cousin Fred and I went along on one of those sales trips. My parents met the train bringing the campers back to the city on one of its stops, and I joined them along with my aunt and cousin, traveling to various small towns and villages. The adults left in the morning for their calls on potential customers and returned in late afternoon. Fred and I stayed at inns during the day. I was bored and lonely and wished I were back at summer camp. Fred was more cheerful. He especially enjoyed traveling from one town to another, stopping in a different inn practically every second night, and staying in a new room. He often taunted me that the room he shared with his mother was more attractive than the one I stayed in with my parents. Although my mother and my aunt would have liked to work regularly, other than on those trips, they had no opportunity to use their working talents. How much they enjoyed the contact with the public! And the self-esteem that they acquired as a result of their earning ability was apparent from their lively discussions in the evening. However, these conversations about their fulfilling day and the wholesome weariness at their return to the inn left me once more feeling lonely and neglected.

As I was growing up, I often felt deprived of a close relationship with a grandparent. I was especially sad not to have
known my grandmother, of whom my mother spoke so lov-
ingly. I was told that she had come as a young girl to Vienna
from Hungary (then part of the Austro-Hungarian Empire);
she had been very pious, was a meticulous homemaker, and
had a beautiful voice that many of her children and grandchildren inherited. Also, she could dance a wild czardas,
usually with Aunt Regin's first husband, who came from
Hungary too. My mother often sang the many melodies of
this Hungarian folk dance that my grandmother danced so
well. I envied my siblings, who had known and loved her.
My father's parents who had died at a much younger age,
never knew my father's children. Still, all of my grandparents died of natural causes. Even though I feel a sense of
deprivation, at least I know that they died before they could
be murdered in a concentration camp.

My father, my sister, and my brother were with Opapa when
he died. I distinctly remember when all three returned home
and my being shocked when I saw Herta's face drained of all
color, white as a sheet: she had witnessed death. This scene
is unforgettable. It was the first time that I saw the effect of
an experience of immense emotional impact. My father tried
to soften the news with philosophical, soothing words to
my mother and Aunt Pepi, saying to them *"der Vater hat die
Mutter gefolgt. Er hat sie getroffen, sie sind zusammen."* That
is, my grandfather had followed my grandmother, who had
died twelve years earlier, and they had met and were now
reunited.

*But wait! Didn't Herta use similar words, four years later, in
her postcard from Auschwitz?*

Yes! That's right, it occurred to me just now! When I recall
these same words in German, I hear the similarity. The Nazis censored everything, and knowing this, she camouflaged
the message so that they would let it through. She may have
remembered the words that my father spoke the day my
grandfather died and thought we would understand. She

wrote an enigmatic postcard, addressing my parents by their first names as though they were her friends, and said: *"Habe gegen alle Erwatungen Eure Mutter hier getroffen."* (Contrary to all my expectations I met your mother here.)

At the time we didn't understand. We thought she might have found my aunt in the camp. Aunt Pepi had also been caught and deported. It was only many years later that I understood that she meant that she had met death all around her. (See pages 135-137.)

Isn't it amazing that letters were actually sent and received from Auschwitz?

It is indeed remarkable that this postcard reached us. Of course, at the time we were still under the illusion that people were deported to labor camps, slave labor of course, but labor just the same. The Germans wanted to perpetuate this fantasy as long as possible, so they let some mail through. It was only after the Liberation that we found out that they were death camps.

Aunt Pepi as a young women in Vienna circa 1915.

*Why not verify now exactly what she said? You know that
sooner or later you'll have to search all the documents that your
parents saved in that box and left in your care. You know the
letter is there.*

Yes, I know where to find all the letters. Nevertheless, I
shall put off searching the dreaded box until I reach 1945 in
my recollections. I am determined to do it, even though I
shudder at the thought. In the meantime I'll go on recalling
1938 and what followed. As horrible as those years may have
been, they pale in comparison to 1942, the year of the imple-
mentation of the German Final Solution to "the Jewish Question,"[5] to 1944 when Belgium (the country to which we fled
in 1938), was liberated, and to 1945 when the war ended in
Europe.

The day of my grandfather's funeral, my cousin Fred and I
stood on the sidewalk across the street from the building
where my grandfather had lived, at number one *Pfeffer Gasse*.
I saw the casket, a plain wooden box, taken out the front
door and loaded into a horse-drawn hearse. Neither my
cousin nor I went to the cemetery for the burial. My mother
and aunt had said that the younger children should be spared
the emotional stress. Even though that decision concerned
me, their opinions were never explained or discussed with
me, and I learned about them only by overhearing. The less
that children knew, it was thought, the better it was for them;
children didn't need explanations. Besides, during those
dangerous times, it was better to keep the children unin-
formed, because if they didn't know anything, they couldn't
tell anyone anything. It was safer that way. It is astounding
that the adults didn't realize that the child might be listening very carefully to all that was being said. Apparently they
were too preoccupied to give it much thought. At other times,
plans were deliberately kept secret, discussed only in my absence, no doubt to prevent me from fretting. Yet, never receiving an explanation of events and decisions, and never
speaking of the feelings that they engendered, often left me
bewildered, frightened, and lonely. Certainly, I knew that
my family meant well, and I felt gratitude towards my par-

ents. When my grandfather died I knew intuitively that by not taking me to the cemetery, they tried to protect me from sorrow. However, in retrospect, I believe that my cousin and I should not have been left out of this ritual. Although my family was not satisfied with the medical care my grandfather had received, and blamed his passing on the political circumstances, his death was part of the natural life cycle. My grandfather was elderly and died as a result of his illness. Even though it was a sorrowful experience and he was mourned by his family, death was a fact that children could understand.

In later years when my mother was herself elderly, I understood that she had never accepted this philosophical explanation. To her, death was to be denied; it was unjust no matter what the age of the individual. Still, the result of my exclusion from my grandfather's funeral was that his death never stood out in my mind as a paramount experience in my childhood. But it may be that this loss was overshadowed by the horror that followed.

Was there any talk about eulogy, or a rabbi's officiating at the funeral?

I didn't hear of any such talk, and not having been to the funeral, I cannot be certain. With respect to the Jewish clergy, there may have been too great a risk in that political situation. However, I know that my grandfather was buried in the Jewish cemetery next to my grandmother. I also remember that my mother and my aunt were looking for low stools to sit "shivah."[6] I cannot say whether the *shivah* lasted the traditional seven days or only three, especially given the political climate. Although everyone in the family had a very strong Jewish identity, we were not particularly pious. We observed dietary laws on major holidays only, and attended religious services solely then. When my brother refused to go to synagogue and would not fast on *Yom Kippur*, the day of atonement, my father got very angry, but to no avail. At age seventeen, my brother could no longer be forced.

At the left is Aunt Franzi, about nineteen with Helene the author's mother, at about twenty two, in Vienna circa 1916.

Can you recall being in a synagogue?

I remember a very large synagogue where Fred had celebrated his *Bar Mitzvah* shortly before the Nazi takeover. My parents attended High Holiday services in a small synagogue nearby. I remember only playing outside with other children who, like myself, were too young to be required to fast on *Yom Kippur*. On that day, we ate with gusto the lunches our parents had packed for us. Our main connection with Judaism stemmed mostly from my siblings' involvement with *Gordonia,* a Zionist youth organization. Herta was seriously interested and active in the group. Ernst had joined mostly for social reasons, especially for outdoor activities such as skiing, mountain climbing, and camping. He also had many good friends, and being handsome, he was extremely popular with the girls in the organization. As for myself, studying Hebrew, Bible, and Jewish history in my school reinforced my identity. Unfortunately, my formal education in Jewish history and religion stopped after the Nazis forced my school to close. Later, during the years in hiding, I learned a great deal about Christianity, particularly Catholicism, in my convent school in Belgium. My study of Judaism resumed only in my late teens, when I was in the United States.

Shortly after my grandfather's funeral, I was perplexed when I saw strangers coming to look at our furniture. My parents gave no reason and I didn't question their actions. Somehow, I knew not to ask, and as usual I informed myself by listening. I was bewildered and confused, because I sensed that some very important and probably dangerous change in our lives lay ahead. The furniture disappeared room by room. My parents' beautiful mahogany bedroom set sold immediately, as did the rest of the furniture. It was snatched up, they said, since it was at such a low price that it was "given away." As the various rooms emptied, we managed as best we could, sleeping on borrowed mattresses. I soon learned that we were moving to another apartment.

Was there already talk about fleeing the country?

Of course, I sensed the precarious state of our existence,

but my recollection as to when I first heard discussions of actual flight remains vague. I seem to remember hearing about it first in the new apartment. My Aunt Pepi and her son Fred moved in with us. The apartment was in a very large building with a big courtyard, in a street off a broad avenue named Prater Strasse. A Jewish family had left it completely furnished. I am not sure whether they had moved somewhere else or had left Austria, but the father remained in Vienna in order to sell their belongings. My parents and he had agreed that we would live there and sell his furniture in the same manner that we had sold ours. He would stop by periodically to collect the money from what was sold.

I don't know whether that neighborhood was considered safer because fewer Jews lived there; it was also in the district Leopoldstadt. But since my parents had sold their furniture, the move was initially prompted by the prospect of having a furnished apartment for a time.

Did the other tenants know that your family was Jewish?

Perhaps they believed that we were, because they knew the people whose apartment we were subletting. But I can't be certain of how they found out. Very shortly after our arrival, I went into the courtyard with my jump rope. Two lovely little blond girls were there already; they were sisters about a year and a half apart; each one had a jump rope, too. We played together all afternoon and got along famously. Having had no playmates of my age for a long time, I was thrilled with my new friends. However, the following day when I saw them in the courtyard, they would not speak to me. Guessing the reason, I asked them point-blank whether their parents had forbidden them to play with me because I was Jewish. I remember the embarrassed demeanor of these six and seven-year-old girls as they nodded. I don't know how they knew. Had I told them the day before? I had said that we just moved there, but as far as saying that we were Jewish, I can't recall . . ., I may have.

Did your family know about this incident?

I didn't tell them because I thought it unimportant. After

all, whether children were playing or not seemed irrelevant; my parents had more pressing worries. I may also have feared being blamed for talking too much. Yet, I cannot recall with certainty how these little girls found out. Still, my silence left me terribly lonely, and my playmates' rejection devastated me.

What about Herta? Didn't you have enough trust to confide in her ?

She was seldom there during my empty hours. Besides,to my knowledge, members of my family seldom spoke of their inner feelings. Also, at that time my older siblings had the same attitude as the adults did toward the younger children. In short, they considered me only a child who did not understand far-reaching, important situations. Although there was great affection between us, I was for them mostly the little sister who sang and danced, was enjoyed and shown off to friends.

And Fred? You could have confided in him, since he and his mother had moved in with you. He was present all the time.

No, if I had told him anything, he would have teased and blamed me. As the furniture continued to disappear little by little, he and I would fight over who would sleep on the little couch that still remained. At the time we didn't get along very well; he often took advantage of my being so much younger by hitting me. This was frequently a subject of contention between my parents and my aunt, who worshiped her only son. They had moved in with my family because my grandfather had been their provider; after his death, my aunt had lost this material support. For my mother, who liked my aunt very much, although at times they quarreled and disagreed, there was no question as to her sisterly duty.

How strange that you remember what now seem such trivial incidents, whereas you forgot others, much more important episodes of that time.

I suppose what seems trivial now had a very strong impact on me then. In any case, I never forgot that the two little girls had been forbidden to play with me because I was Jew-

The author's parents, Helene and Saly Scheer as a young married couple, circa 1917.

ish, after we had had such a good time together. From that time on, I never told anyone unless I already knew that the other person was Jewish too. Even years later, shortly after our arrival in the United States, I outraged my mother's youngest sister Franzi, who with her family had left Austria for the United States in 1935 (three years before the "Anschluss"). She had found out that I had evaded the question of religion and would not admit voluntarily to being Jewish. At the time I could neither understand nor explain my denial. Though I felt guilty and cowardly, I didn't want to change my attitude.

Another occurrence, which now might appear insignificant but nonetheless stayed imprinted, was a brief incident with my mother. One afternoon I was lying on that same little couch, so often the subject of my disputes with my cousin. My mother was bagging objects that she planned to give away when I noticed her including a small doll, one of my favorite toys. When I protested bitterly and asked for an explanation, her only answer was a very severe look. I understood that look. It meant that I should know without a verbal explanation; I should understand that we were going to leave and could not bring toys along. Even at the time of the incident, I grasped the futility of complaining, and with a heavy heart, insisted no further.

Were Ernst and Herta gone by then? They left Vienna separately from the rest of you. Can you recollect their departure?

I remember only discussions of them leaving before us, and then their absence. Ernst was always taken for a gentile and would get into fights defending Jews from Nazi youths; he often came home bearing the marks of those fights. My parents feared for his safety and were relieved at his departure, although they then fretted about my siblings' dangerous flight as well as their illegal entry into another country.

At that time our daily life was monotonous. I missed the spontaneous singing of my mother and sister, from whom I had learned the old Viennese songs and many tunes from operettas by Johann Strauss and Franz Lehár, to which my mother would sing the harmony. They would break into song while cooking, sewing, or dusting, their beautiful voices resonating in the apartment. True, most of the musical gaiety occurred before the political turmoil; there was very little singing in the present dwelling. However, singing remained always a way of loosening tension, as well as an expression of hope for better times to come. The whole family sang, even those members whose voices were not particularly harmonious. As years went by, however, spontaneous singing dwindled

Through all the lengthy sojourns in different countries, in spite of her animosity toward her native land, my mother always sang those Viennese songs; she never really integrated the new languages, whether French, Spanish, or English, only humming the melodies of the songs she heard in those tongues. I could not understand her lack of interest in the new cultural expressions around us, since I adopted them so enthusiastically. When we escaped to Belgium, I quickly grew familiar with our new culture. Little by little I rejected all that had to do with the country from which we fled. Although I never really forgot the songs and the music and found them beautiful, I finally denied them and turned toward the sounds of my new culture. My childish discernment was too limited to comprehend my mother's dilemma. I was young enough to escape the imprinting of a past that was difficult to erase for someone who had known happy days growing up in that past. As so often in life, meaning clarifies with age, when frequently it is too late to lend comfort and understanding. Still, psychological motives or predicaments were never explored or discussed in the family, and that was a pity. Such deliberations would have been comforting to us all. As I grew up, I always blamed my sense of isolation on having lacked the company of children my age. Decades later I understood that our not speaking of our inner lives was what made me feel isolated.

Ernst, twelve years my senior, never got over the hurt of having to flee. Once during a conversation four decades later, the subject came up regarding life's greatest disillusions. I asked him what he considered his biggest disappointment. Since I never identified with anything Austrian, I was amazed when he said that his greatest distress in life stemmed from having to flee what he had considered his home, and that for many years he cried each time he saw mountains, because they reminded him of the many hikes in the Austrian countryside.

So Ernst and Herta had left; did they communicate from Belgium?

My memory of the time after their departures is very murky. I cannot remember hearing anyone speak of any letters from them. However, I sensed that our own emigration was imminent. We left carrying no luggage whatsoever, in order not to attract attention. On the morning that we set out, we all dressed in several layers of underwear and socks; I wore all of my three favorite dresses. A small tear in the lining of my coat inspired my mother to hide in it some money in bills. I had heard the adults saying that each person was allowed to take only a small amount of money out of the country, with a threat of severe penalty for anyone disobeying this rule. I distinctly recall the unease I felt in observing my mother's action. I mentally questioned the wisdom of her gesture, especially after seeing the safety pin used to make a hasty repair. I had heard that people were searched, and I suspected that this money would easily be found. She must have thought that a child would not be searched very thoroughly; I vaguely recall her saying so in the excitement and anticipation of our departure. I remember thinking that this decision was made in haste, not sufficiently considered. Still, I also recall feeling that I was very inexperienced and that my mother must know best, so I said nothing.

You left with your parents, Aunt Pepi, and your cousin Fred. How did you reach the border ?

I recall being in a train compartment, sitting across from my mother. She was trying to make light of our predica-

The author with brother Ernst, Vienna 1938.

ment by saying in a self-deprecating, falsetto voice - her custom when she was joking - *"wir sind jezt arme Emigranten "'* (we are now poor emigrants). I am uncertain whether this train ride took place before coming to the Austrian border or after having crossed it. However, I remember very distinctly the circumstances at the Austrian customhouse.

Was there still a border between Austria and Germany? Did not the "Anschluss" unite these countries into one?

That is so, it was all Germany then, yet I had always thought of it as the Austrian border. Also following that experience, I recall being in Germany proper from where we had to cross into Holland before passing that border into Belgium. I remember that papers were examined, and my parents and aunt had to sign documents pledging never to return. We were searched for money, jewels, or other valuables in excess of what the authorities granted each individual.[7] Again, all my information came from listening to the adults' discussions. I heard them complaining about such a paltry sum and fearing that such meager resources surely destined all emigrants to indigence. In short, the fleeing Jews were forced to leave all their possessions behind. At that moment, we were lucky to have escaped with our lives.

Although some of my recollections are shadowy, the ordeal at that customhouse always remained vivid. It was the first in a series of horrendous experiences of my childhood; it was a trial where all my accumulated anguish reached its zenith.

Were the personnel hostile? What exactly do you remember?

The men and the women were searched by clerks of their own gender. My mother, my aunt, and I had to strip. The woman examiner was not unfriendly; she was just following orders, just doing her job. She examined every piece of clothing very thoroughly. When she inspected my coat, she came upon the safety pin that held the tear in the lining. Since the forbidden money hidden there had made me uncomfortable all along, I remember carefully observing her facial expression. It seemed to me then that the safety pin roused her suspicion. Manipulating the lining, it was easy to feel the bills, and loosening the safety pin, she extracted the money. She also found a valuable jeweled metal pencil that my mother carried in her purse. However, the gravest offense was the money hidden in my coat. I clearly remembered the warning that any attempt to remove from the country more money than the allotted amount would be met with the gravest consequences, and I was petrified.

The woman could not be persuaded to keep her findings secret, even when she was offered the money. My mother and aunt begged her to say nothing; she replied she couldn't, because she would be dismissed if found out. We dressed and followed her into the main office. A very tall SS officer with thinning, sandy blond hair was waiting, self-assured and powerful in that black uniform that I found so terrifying, the swastika on his arm band so threatening. My father and my cousin were already there. The woman put the money and jeweled pencil on a counter where the officer stood, and then left. Seeing her discoveries, he exploded; *"Was! So eine Schweinerei!"* (What! Such filthiness!) The translation depicts the general meaning. Yet, the German term contains the word "pig" so that the translation of "Schweinerei" does not render the full impact of the expression, nor does it communicate the screaming sound of the combination of consonants and vowels in German. The man's voice sharpened. He added hissingly: *"Wissen Sie, Sie können verhaftet werden?"* (Do you know, you can be arrested?)

Because no "illegal" money was found on Aunt Pepi and Fred, they were allowed to leave, and I became more terrified. Since the money was found in my coat, I was convinced that I was guilty and that something horrible was going to happen to me. And, being my parents' child, they would be held as accomplices. Hysterical, I sobbed out of control. Annoyed at my crying, the SS man snapped toward my mother, *"Beruhigen Sie das Kind"* (Calm the child).

Did she purposely not say anything to you, thinking that your sobbing might dim his anger?

Until just now, I never considered that a possibility. I remember her glancing at me furtively, but she said nothing. I think she was too preoccupied, and although frightened, she argued with him slightly. It was again her "Aryan" appearance that then gave her such aplomb; my father remained silent, and I continued to sob wildly. She may have had no plan, but her not consoling me worked in the end. After questioning my parents for what seemed an eternity, the officer may have been so annoyed at my outburst that he gave orders to let me go. I met my aunt and cousin waiting in the street. After a while my parents were able to leave the customhouse, too. The Nazi scheme was not yet in full gear in 1938. In short, all of us were lucky that time.

How can you explain your quieting down immediately after meeting Aunt Pepi and Fred, while your mother and father were still being held? Didn't you worry about them?

I clearly recall the sensation of being released from certain doom. The money had been found in my coat, therefore I was the most guilty, yet they let me go. In retrospect, I assume that my childish optimism trusted in the ability of my parents, and most probably in some sense of justice. If I, the most guilty one, was allowed to leave, they also would be let go. Had I had the maturity of an adult, I could have been spared the guilt feelings engendered by my aunt's mocking astonishment at my sudden calm after being set free, even though my parents were still being held. I worried about her telling them, and she did so, in a light, satirical fashion when my parents joined us. I was very troubled and can recall watching my mother's face; she smiled and seemed surprised, but said nothing. There was no time to dwell on useless matters.

My resentment of my aunt's insensitivity remained through my childhood, so did deep feelings of guilt for not having worried enough about my parents. Besides, I was deeply hurt at Aunt Pepi's apparently spiteful remarks. Although I never expressed my feelings to anyone, I always recalled that incident.

My memory is cloudy about what exactly followed. I still recollect my anguish at seeing threatening, long swastika flags waving from stately buildings. It was a cool gray day, and I was on the sidewalk of a street in a city that the adults called Cologne, and then we had to travel to Aachen before reaching the Dutch border. Later, I was in the kitchen of a private house, watching an older woman washing dishes at a sink in front of two windows. We had crossed the Dutch border; the house was in Maastricht. Sunlight flowed through the windows; the woman spoke to me in Dutch, which I didn't understand, but her tone was friendly and she smiled. However, I was intimidated by her looks. I was very aware that her thin jet-black hair was dyed; it conflicted with her wrinkled complexion. The fact that the woman sheltered refugees for the night for a price - included in our smuggler's deal - made me suspicious.

However, my feelings of distress were not as acute then as earlier. Perhaps the plain, private house, the sunny kitchen, and the friendly woman communicated a sense of home and thus reduced my insecurity. In spite of my misgivings, I had a sense of alliance with the woman of the house and later with the two guides who smuggled us over the Belgian border. It gave me confidence to know that these people were engaged in our clandestine journey. In addition, the absence of swastika flags and Nazi uniforms, constant symbols of danger and hostility, lessened considerably my feelings of doom. Nevertheless, I was keenly aware of our precarious situation. This was a hiding place, and although at that time Jews were not persecuted in Holland, we were in the country unlawfully, and because we had no visas, we could be sent back if found out by the authorities.

I was much less frightened, even later when separated from my parents for the illegal border crossing into Belgium. I recall no strong anxiety during that episode. I don't remember seeing any streets, only that house, and later, under the cover of darkness, the countryside where we met with our guides.

What was the purpose of having the children cross the border separately? Didn't it increase the level of everyone's anxiety?

I suppose that the adults had confidence in the guides. We were assured of a better chance of success and of being reunited on the Belgian side of the border. Our faith in our parents and their reliance on the advice of the guides relieved my anxiety. Also, my cousin was in good humor, and excited at the thought of crossing a frontier clandestinely. It may have reminded him of some detective story he had read and enlivened his sense of adventure, especially since we were going by car.

Now the logic of the two guides could be understood; one guide took the adults and the other, the children. Fred and I sat in the back seat of the vehicle; I believe it was a taxi. We were advised to duck down right before the border, so that the car would appear to have no passengers, and we were not to sit up until told to. The ride took about ten or fifteen minutes. Dark fields bordered each side of the road. When in the distance our guide identified the light of the custom's booth, we ducked down as told. Looking up from the floor as we drove across the border, we noticed that the driver, who had rolled down the window, waved amicably and shouted greetings to the custom's agent standing in front of the booth, who in turn signaled for him to drive on. Shortly after having been given permission to sit up, we were taken to a spot in the fields where we met our parents. They had taken a shortcut and had crossed on foot. I especially remember my mother's face; she was smiling, showing relief and hope. Fred was delighted with our crossing and kept relating every detail, especially about how cleverly our driver had tricked the border guard.

The period of childhood enables a dangerous and threatening situation to be metamorphosed into an exciting adventure, as it was for Fred. In retrospect, this could have turned out to be a disaster. We might have been separated from our parents forever. Our fate could have been similar to that of so many other children. Either group, on our separate ways, could have been stopped and sent back. The destiny of separated parents and children who failed to escape has been well documented.[8] These children never saw their parents again.

Unfortunately, that same appreciation for adventure may have been instrumental four years later, when at age seventeen Fred was lured with two of his closest friends, as were so many thousands of other young people, to answer willingly the Nazi summons for "work."

CHAPTER II

REFUGEES

Brussels, Belgium: our new environment and our living quarters stand out clearly in my memory.

In the late summer of 1938 we lived in the *commune* of *Anderlecht,* a district of the city of Brussels, in a lower-middle-class and working-class area inhabited by small shop keepers, as well as white-collar and blue-collar workers. It was also a Jewish neighborhood. The gray-faced houses were mainly of equal height with their slanted roofs punctuated by garret windows. On the corner of *Rue de l'Instruction* and *Boulevard de la Révision* stood a *brasserie,* one of the many beer salons so popular in Belgium, then also euphemistically called *café.* A tree lined strip of land, dotted with benches, ran through the middle of the *Boulevard,* which was favored by the many animal lovers in the neighborhood for exercising their dogs.

We lived on the fourth floor of that corner house, right under the roof. My sister lived somewhere else, but my brother Ernst's garret was next to ours, and across the hall was the one shared by my aunt Pepi and my cousin Fred. The whitewashed rooms were small and sparsely equipped with old furniture; each room contained an iron double bed, a table and four chairs, and a small wardrobe. A rickety wooden stand held a large ceramic basin and a water jug for washing, and next to it was a large iron bucket for collecting liquid waste. In one corner stood a little coal-burning stove, and on a shelf sat a *réchaud,* a portable gas stove with two burners. Since little light penetrated through the small slanted attic window, the naked electric bulb hanging overhead had to remain on, especially on cloudy days.

There was another, much larger garret on the floor that belonged to Monsieur Roussell. Time had effaced the name of this old gentleman, but it suddenly came back to me by strong concentration. I had never before written his name, and the spelling may not be correct, but it reflects the intonation. I remember him well - he was a kind, worldly Frenchman probably in his late seventies. In stark contrast to our walls which were so white and bare, the walls of his spacious room were covered with faded blue-flowered wallpaper. It was the only wallpapered room on the attic floor. I found it so well appointed! An injured veteran of World War I, Monsieur Roussell walked with the help of a cane. He befriended us, and we were able to communicate because he spoke German. He often advised my aunt and my mother where to shop at the lowest prices, where wood for kindling was 10 *centimes* less per kilo and was drier; wood was often sold wet to increase its weight. This kindly man lived on his pension from the French government and had to watch his *centimes* carefully.

There were rodents in the building, mostly mice, especially in the attic floor. However, on one occasion on my way downstairs, I met a rat the size of a small cat; it looked up at me as if surprised at the sound of my scream and scurried away. But it was caught immediately and disposed of because I turned and ran back up to tell Monsieur Roussell, who was usually in his room. He alerted the *patronne* (manager) of the *café,* a fortyish hefty Flemish woman who also collected the rents from the tenants of the building. I often heard her rough laughter and loud arguments with her customers. Her coarseness intimidated me. Behind the safely closed door of our garret room, I heard her and her young handyman whacking the rat as they shouted in Flemish. When the commotion ceased, I knew that for the time being, I needn't fear taking the stairs down to the street. This rat was gone.

My mother and my aunt desperately tried to destroy the bedbugs as they frantically sprayed with petroleum the iron bed frames and springs of the bolsters, which served at the time as box springs. Although the vermin and rodents disturbed me, given my childish optimism, I was not overly depressed by the sad surroundings. I was mostly saddened by my mother's severe back pain which often kept her bedridden. This ailment corrected itself, and in later years she forgot having experienced it. However, having to share the bed with my parents distressed me immensely.

I never knew whether Fred also objected to sharing his bed with his mother - he was thirteen years old by then. Again, feelings were never discussed. Besides my cousin and I still were not very close, so we would not confide in each other. But I overheard the adults, and especially my sister, objecting to this arrangement. My parents would silently nod. Nevertheless, I perceived that my mother did not think it so bad; she thought of Fred as still very young. I never heard my aunt or my cousin discuss the matter, but thought they did not mind. I recall reflecting about it, since I found sharing my parents' bed so objectionable for myself. My own attitude clearly indicated my resentment of my lack of privacy. Yet I anticipated a reprimand if I voiced my objection, especially by my father who at the time was very impatient with what he considered sensitive nonsense. I recognized the constraining circumstances that compelled us to live in such poor housing, and I realized that I was expected to understand. Still, discussing the subject would have helped me to adjust to this unaccustomed and sad environment.

Were these accommodations the family's choice because Ernst lived there already? Who chose these meager lodgings for you?

Ernst was the reconnoiterer, since he had arrived first. For the sake of expediency and because rooms were available there, we moved into the same building without looking elsewhere. Lists of inexpensive housing were provided by *Le*

Comité des Refugiés (Committee for Refugees), a Jewish agency set up to provide help and social services for Jews fleeing Nazi persecution. The low rent had determined Ernst's choice of his lodging. We followed the same pattern because our resources were so very limited. Herta found work as a domestic with a family, earning room and board besides some pocket money.

You knew that Herta was very unhappy there.

Yes, I was aware of her dejection. When several years later I questioned my father, I found that her depression had been due essentially to the way she was treated by the family for whom she worked, rather than to the job itself. Although such work was considered the lowest kind and an affront to Jewish middle-class social values, Herta was practical and philosophical about her situation. She knew that her hopes of attaining the prestigious teaching profession would have to be set aside for the foreseeable future. A sweet and docile person, she cried but still accepted the situation because there was no alternative. However, she had displayed a knack for sewing since her early teens, and she was soon able to benefit from this skill. When an opportunity presented itself, she took the option of working as a seamstress in an *atelier de confection*, a sewing workshop making ready-to-wear clothes.

Did the Belgian authorities issue working permits and grant refugees permission to earn salaries?

In the spring of 1938 the arrival of refugees in the country was illegal. Ernst and his friends told fearful stories of escaping over the rooftops of buildings from plainclothesmen searching for illegal foreigners. Shortly after our arrival, the government allowed legal stay to refugees who could prove that for the time being they were simply in transit, just waiting to proceed to another destination. I recall that on one occasion when I was sent to buy bread, two men entered the bakery and asked worried customers, obviously foreigners, for identification. Having already completed my purchase I hurried out, conscious of the need to appear "normal," and

I was relieved at hearing the sound of the little bell attached to the door as it closed behind me. Investigations occurred in many ordinary situations in neighborhoods that were well known to harbor refugees.

When did your family's stay become legal in Belgium? Of course, at the time you may not have been cognizant of the change of status..

Yet even at age eight, I was keenly aware of all incidents. We most likely had a temporary authorization, since we thought of ourselves in transit. My parents must have had some documents from the American immigration authorities testifying to my mother's younger sister Franzi's attempt to bring us to Ohio. I conclude this because I was never given instructions to avoid or to fear the Belgian authorities. Some months later I witnessed with my father an occurrence similar to the one in the bakery. It must have been in late autumn for I remember him in his winter coat and brown hat on a gloomy, rainy afternoon. We were in an establishment where policemen in plain clothes demanded to see everyone's papers. Commotion ensued. Since new refugees kept fleeing Nazi persecution, some of the newcomers who were present may not as yet have been able to obtain legal status. Confidently my father submitted his identification for inspection. *Ça va, c'est bien* (it's all right), muttered the official impassively. My worry must have been evident, for my father smiled and nodded reassuringly; then with his hand on my shoulder, we walked out of the room.

Le Comité des Refugiés[9] helped with finding housing for immigrants, but the authorities denied emigrés the privilege of working. Therefore, financial assistance was the principal purpose of the Jewish community in founding the *Comité*. Consequently, every refugee acquired a small sum for living expenses. It was difficult, however, to subsist on such a meager allowance. Some people risked illegal employment and deportation if found out. I overheard many discussions concerning the exploitation of illegal workers by employers who paid them shamefully low wages. These discussions took

place among acquaintances, many formerly business owners seeking to place themselves temporarily in light manufacturing, such as ready to wear clothes, leather goods, and
furs. People often took piecework home in order to avoid
being apprehended in workshops.

Members of my family may have worked illegally, too. I
don't know whether Herta's job was legal then. My father
was knowledgeable about fabrics and cloth manufacturing;
eventually, he too worked at cutting and sewing ready-to-
wear clothes and subsequently furs. Three years later at age
sixteen, Fred worked with leather goods. Although far from
satisfactory and considered below the accustomed Jewish
middle-class standard, these jobs helped alleviate a substan-
dard existence. Ernst said that he would work only in draft-
ing or construction. He may have worked illegally before he
left the country in 1939 for South America.

Some warm sensations and bright images of that time linger on, the dreary memories notwithstanding. These impressions resulted from the sense of identity and family, and
the nearness of loved ones. Also, in spite of all the agitation,
my mother's strength was central to this very unity. Clearly,
her mental as well as her physical condition always influenced my own outlook. My own level of anxiety rose or fell
according to my perception of hers. Moreover, we experienced a somewhat hopeful time then. First of all, the expectation that we would go to the United States to join my
mother's younger sister and her family ruled our thoughts
and fueled our hopes. In addition, I enjoyed the presence
and support of an extended family. Besides my parents and
siblings, my Aunt Pepi and my cousin, Brussels harbored for
a short time various friends and relatives, some of whom I
had heard of but had never met. A prime example was my
cousin Max, the younger of my mother's oldest sister Regin's
two sons, for whom I had great affection. He was then probably twenty-two or twenty-three years old, tall and handsome, gentle, generous, and sunny. Max had fled to Belgium from Czechoslovakia. I admired his beautifully
schooled singing and his dancing talents. He had been a

semiprofessional in Prague, where he had trained in flamenco dancing and in voice. It had been difficult for him to earn a proper income from such performances, and so he chose interior decorating as his primary profession. As I think of it now, this additional expertise explains his refined taste and elegance. He was a frequent visitor, and on occasion he came with his girlfriend Sadie, a young Belgian Jewish woman. Young people's ages were often a subject of discussion between my mother and aunt and I listened attentively. That's how I knew that Sadie was older than Max. Sadie was also one of Herta's friends. Another of our frequent visitors was my sister's former boyfriend Walter Simoni, from her Zionist youth group, *Gordonia*. We liked him very much and were sorry that she had lost interest in him. He remained a close friend of the family.

Eduard, my mother's older brother and his family joined us in Brussels several months after our arrival. His Aryan wife Mia and their eleven year old daughter Sonia, followed him into exile.

Was your uncle Eduard protected in Vienna because of his Aryan wife, and had this situation delayed their flight?

I never heard anyone say that this was the case. However, their daughter obtained some privileges from persecution in Belgium several years later during the German occupation. Yet at the time of the *Anschluss*, from the Nazis' point of view, divorce was the only path for an Aryan's rehabilitation from *Rassenschande* (race disgrace). Regin, my mother's oldest sister, and her gentile husband fled from Munich around that time. They were the most fortunate in the family, for they reached London and thereby escaped Nazi persecution.

The presence of Eduard's family always created friction and unease. Why was this?

The reasons were mainly related to Mia. I recollect hearing that she had promised to become Jewish when she married Eduard. I don't know whether she actually converted. However, I recall the celebrations of Christian holidays and customs in their home in Vienna, especially Saint Nicholas and

Standing first on the right is Uncle Eduard in the Austrian army
in World War I.

Christmas. I remember the Christmas tree and my cousin Sonia's boasting about the merits of that holiday in comparison with what she and her mother thought about Chanukah. The family resented these celebrations; they considered the wife and daughter outsiders and Eduard a weakling. Mia prevailed: adamant, opinionated, and aggressive, she continued to celebrate the Christian holidays. Although she may have at times wanted a more harmonious rapport with her husband's family, both sides were responsible for a mainly lukewarm relationship; she always stayed the *Schikse* (gentile unmarried woman).

Well then, you can hardly say that these relatives added any sense of solidarity. Rather, it seems that they injected divisiveness; how can it be that their company enhanced your feeling of security?

Even though the tendency toward discord often lay just beneath the surface, still their presence was welcome, because it transmitted some form of comfort. Perhaps it was the solace that after all, they too were safe. Whatever the disagreement and lack of affinity, they were family. On the other hand, since quarrels are often common in families and had occurred in the past in ours, the occasional discord may have provided an appearance of normalcy.

Your affection for this cousin Sonia was minimal.

She was three and a half years older, a considerable difference when one is eight years old. In addition, the cultural division separated us, especially under the circumstances. Her marked preference for Christian holidays while ignoring Jewish ones disturbed me. Besides, both the mother's and the daughter's haughty manner and superior attitude were hurtful and irritating.

Don't forget the feeling of competition in your artistic endeavors.

Yes, I found her toe dancing most enviable, more desirable than my own acting and singing. On the other hand, I also admired her talents. In retrospect, the sense of rivalry was mostly fueled by both sets of parents.

Forcing childhood memories out of the shadows unveils long-forgotten personalities. Remarkably, I suddenly remembered this other regular visitor. But who was he? It seems that I was able to recall his name by sheer force of will. My evoking images and events at which he was present triggered the memory, just as I had previously remembered, after fifty years, our garret neighbor Monsieur Roussell. This man's name was Robert, and he was about twenty-five, and from Vienna too. I had never met him before. He was a grandson of my grandfather's younger brother, thus a second cousin to my mother. I recall the sound of that name pronounced by the family in German, with the emphasis on the first syllable and the open "o." In my mind I can now see his face, his fair complexion, his blue eyes, and even the dark gray, double-breasted suit that he always wore. Although he was tall and well built, I didn't consider him handsome like my cousin Max. In retrospect, my opinion was probably influenced by the adults' view of his meekness which was not regarded as a manly quality.

But Max was soft and gentle, too, yet you thought him handsome.

Yes, and so did my mother and my aunt who also admired his artistic talents; no doubt this view had some bearing on my sentiment. Nevertheless, although I favored Max, I liked Robert too and enjoyed his presence.

Thus, for a short time, although I was always the youngest child and mostly surrounded by adults, I was nevertheless free of the loneliness I had experienced earlier. I was often pampered, usually by my siblings and their many friends, especially by Ernst's many girlfriends, for he was quite the lady's man. My brother's success with young women became legendary.

But then it no longer worried your mother.

No, maternal suspicion was no longer an issue. On the

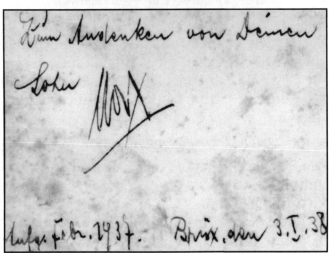

Cousin Max Glasz,
"A memento from your son, Max
"Photographed Feb, 1937. Brussells, Jan. 3, 1938"
Max sent this pictuer to his mother who was still in Munich.

contrary, my mother laughingly boasted about Ernst's popularity, the subject of everyone's amusement and of no one's disapproval. But, I never heard him boasting of his many conquests. In spite of my affection for him, I felt uneasy about such behavior. I was disturbed that there seemed to be a double standard for men and women and that a young man's amorous intrepidity inspired esteem. However, although it made me uneasy, I thought that such conduct on the part of unmarried men was normal and acceptable, since no one objected. In addition, I enjoyed the company of these young women, who for a short period of time came to see him. I met each one at different times. My favorites were two gentile Belgian girls. Shortly after our arrival, I met the blond Adrienne. Somehow I drew a parallel between her and the day outside, feeling that she brightened the gloomy room in the same way as the ray of sunlight coming through the attic window. Her relationship with my brother was brief; I saw her only twice. I am not certain of the other Belgian girl's name, but I think it was Gabrielle.

Better not guess. Remember that even then you confused their names, and Ernst corrected you.

True, strangely enough I forgot Gabrielle's name just as I did when I was eight years old, although she was one of my favorites. As with Adrienne, I met her also shortly after our arrival in Brussels. Ernst had said that she would come to take me out.

How did you and Gabrielle communicate ?

I recall that we understood each other. There was a feeling of affinity between us. As yet I knew no French then, so she must have known some German. We stopped at an automatic chocolate dispenser, something very new to me. I understood perfectly when she asked me to choose, although I don't know whether she spoke French or German, probably a mixture of both. Again I remember this taking place on a bright day. In retrospect, it seems that there was a correspondence between the environment and my state of mind. In other words, the sunshine, the friendly girl's shiny dark hair, her white blouse and printed skirt, the lively city street, all instilled in me feelings of comfort and contentment. And, of course, the chocolate was a great treat! What made it more wonderful was my sensing her own pleasure. In addition, I knew that we were having lunch at her house so I anticipated that this first indulgence was only a preliminary of further happy events.

Yet, what comes to mind is your singing, rather than what was served there. Again, how did you make yourself understood?

I felt very much at ease with both the daughter and the mother. Although the mother and I did not communicate verbally, I sensed warm interest on her part and much affinity between us. I recall a very soft, expressive face. Furthermore, in stark contrast to my family's present situation and our dismal lodgings, images and sensations of comfort, permanence, and stability emanated from this home. An upright piano stood along a wall in the dining room. After we finished lunch the young woman sat down at the piano and encouraged me to sing. She knew of my singing because Ernst always spoke of it to his friends. Of course, I obliged gladly. She followed me, playing by ear the melodies of parts of the operettas of Strauss and Lehár that I had heard my mother and sister sing, as well as popular songs I had heard my siblings and their friends play on records. At a time of acute feelings of insecurity and instability, this very pleasant experience remained indelible. Yet, the positive sensations experienced through that relationship were short lived. I never saw either of the young women again. Ernst became seriously involved with Rachelle, who was not my favorite, but I don't remember ever voicing my preference to him. I thought Rachelle was pretty. She was tall and slender, with shoulder length sandy- blond hair and blue eyes, but I found her lacking in warmth toward children. Probably she seemed distant because she didn't fuss over me the way everybody else did. Her aloofness may have sent the wrong signal. Yet, her attitude gave her a certain air of dignity. It was clear that she was no one's fool, and Ernst knew it. She wouldn't have tolerated sharing his affection or attention with his other girlfriends.

You also must acknowledge that you understood and appreciated the fact that she was also very useful.

I admit that besides understanding that the choice was my brother's, I intuitively recognized Rachelle's many qualities. First of all, Rachelle was Jewish, and that was very important. However, I sensed from my mother's attitude that the family considered Ernst too young and the circumstances too uncertain for him to be seriously involved. Also, they felt that his romances were ephemeral. But, no one ever objected to his friendships, since everyone knew that he would disregard any interference. I assume that the family appreciated Rachelle's being Jewish. Yet I never heard them say so. I just knew it, felt it, no discussion was needed. Another quality I intuitively understood about her was that she worked for the *Comité des Réfugiés*. Although only twenty years old, she had an influential job with access to information that was crucial. She knew who was able to apply for aid and the best way to go about it; she could obtain information regarding government policies toward immigrants; and she had access to newly available visas to countries out of Europe. Her position there may have initiated Ernst's interest, but soon he became very smitten with her. She may have been instrumental in providing Ernst's opportunity to be among a small group of young men to leave Europe for South America in 1939.

I never saw my sister and Rachelle spending time together. I don't think they disliked each other, but I believe there was not enough similarity between them for a close friendship. I sensed a certain coolness on Rachelle's part; that may have been one of the reasons for my ambiguous feelings toward her.

Wasn't Rachelle also an influence in your brief career on the Yiddish stage?

I never considered that possibility before writing this. If I had thought of it at all, I would have attributed the influence to her father. Indeed, failing to acknowledge Rachelle was thoughtless and unjust. She brought me home to meet her parents, and subsequently I was often there for dinner and became her father's protegee. He was an amateur impresario and an agent. However, my first opportunities in Brussels for acting and singing came about during the celebrations of Jewish festivals organized by the *Comité*. The organization provided the Brussels refugee community with most of its social life. The program was especially extensive for children. As in previous years, the Jewish festivals were the time to shine. This was especially true in 1938 when the celebration of Chanukah lightened an otherwise grim winter. Cousin Sonia participated in the Chanukah celebrations at the *Comité*. In retrospect, I believe that then they participated in all celebrations, Jewish and Christian. This practice was frowned upon by my family then and not considered sincere.

What prompted you to start singing in Yiddish? After all, you didn't speak it and it was not a language held in high esteem among members of your family or their circle of friends.

Regrettably, among many German-speaking Jews, Yiddish was not regarded as a real language. It was thought of as an adulterated, deformed low German, the jargon of backward Jews from Eastern Europe. Yet, everyone often used Yiddish expressions. Words such as *meshuga, nebich,* and *mies* (crazy, mischance, homely) represented global Jewish idioms, but they were only whispered outside the home. We were amazed to hear from Ernst, shortly after we arrived, that a song with Yiddish words was in vogue in Brussels. Everyone sang *"Bei mir bist du schein,"* and it could even be heard often on the radio. I didn't know that it was sung by the Andrew Sisters, that it was American, and that only the first line was in Yiddish, but that was not important then. Our bewilderment stemmed from the democratic freedom in Belgium. It was amazing to us that a song with Yiddish words was played in nightclubs, that people danced to it, and that it was heard on the radio! Some of the young refugees even went so far as to see a Yiddish aspect to the "Lambeth Walk," an American tune and dance style in vogue then as well.

How did they imagine that there was a resemblance? Did they even understand the English lyrics?

No one really understood. What struck them as Yiddish was that in the dance, at the end of the stanza when the dancers spun, they gestured with the thumb pointing backwards (the way one would hitchhike) and exclaimed *"pey!"* (instead of *"hey,"* which I heard many years later). As always, I mimicked my siblings, singing the melody and imitating the English sounds.

Yiddish seemed much more accepted in Belgium, but I felt ill at ease in that language. My uncle Eduard especially derided those songs, and he made me feel ridiculous singing them. No matter how successful my performances and how great my parents' pride, that sense of ridicule could not be shaken. It took me decades to overcome those feelings.

At the first Chanukah performance at the *Comité*, I sang the one and only Yiddish song I knew and had learned before our arrival in Brussels. *"Der Chalutz"* was a story of a young Zionist boy arriving in Tel Aviv. Herta sang it in her youth group, *Gordonia*. I picked it up as with all the songs I heard around me. Somehow this song suited me, especially because it could be performed rather than just sung. No one on the Yiddish stage in Brussels had heard it before, and it became one of my stage trademarks. That was the very song Eduard mocked so often. He would say to me, distorting the words and grinning sarcastically, "Sing : *ich pak schoen mein paekel,"* (I am packing my bundle), a line from the song. Yiddish was a big joke, in the extreme even regarded in bad taste and never considered worthy in connection with any art form.

Did Eduard's wife and daughter mock you too?

Not with words, but their sarcasm was noticeable in their body language and in their obviously suppressed smiles. I never discussed this with anyone. As always, feelings were never examined, and I informed myself by listening to discussions. The rest of the family attributed their attitude to envy. This view may have been conveyed to me personally, but I have no clear recollection of such an occasion. In fact, I doubted my family's sincerity. I had heard similar derogatory remarks from my mother and Aunt Pepi on previous occasions, but not from Herta. I mistrusted their sudden change in attitude, which seemed to me adopted for expediency's sake. An undeniable dislike had been instilled in me, and it was as though suddenly I was told to think that Yiddish was fine, that it was entertaining, even beautiful. Too bad that no one could comprehend the necessity of an explanation. A clear and simple elucidation of former and present sentiments would have solved the problem. An explanation that even adults could change their mind, could learn to appreciate in earnest what had been mocked before, would have relieved my ambivalence. Later I knew that in fact there was a change of mind. Unfortunately, at the time the necessity of probing children's' sentiments did not occur to them, I doubt whether they even thought it worthy to examine their own. Herta was sentimental and introspective, and she most probably had such discussions with her friends, but never within my earshot.

Herta inherited these characteristics from my father. But my father's propensity for self-examination and feeling became evident to me only in my adulthood. Although very loving, he was, during my childhood, at times a severe and occasionally an unreasonable disciplinarian. However, he delighted in my stage career. At some point he was also involved in the business aspect of the performance in 1939 when I participated with several artists in an evening of Jewish music. The concert was held in a rented hall named *La Maison de Huit Heures*, located in the center of Brussels. Since my father had no money, he could contribute only work, so he cooperated in the planning and the publicity. Rachelle's father knew all the entrepreneurs of the Yiddish stage and did not approve of this show's principal organizer. Nevertheless, he joined in the effort when my father was promised 3 percent of the take. Perhaps 3 percent wasn't very much, but that is the figure I remember hearing. Rachelle's last name was Herchlikovitz (I am spelling it literally). This is another name that I miraculously succeeded in recalling by force of concentration over several days. It sprung out of the past from a forty-five-year shadow. When Rachelle's father was the subject of conversation, no one ever mentioned his first name. He was always *der Herchlikovitz* who furnished me with most of my repertoire. He taught me many Yiddish songs when I was over at their home for dinner. His wife would help out, calling from the kitchen when he forgot the lyrics. Because he had no sheet music, everything was transmitted from memory. Their daughter Hélène, Rachelle's slightly younger sister, played the notes out on the piano, searching for the right melody, writing the music phrase by phrase as she listened and played. Rachelle could play as well and accompanied me occasionally.

How did you communicate with Rachelle's father at first, before you knew French?

We managed between his Yiddish and my German. In fact, I picked up Yiddish easily from him. At the time I never noticed any problems. However, several months later, when he expressed his relief at our finally being able to speak French, I learned that he had indeed found communicating with me to be difficult.

He also made sure that I wouldn't infringe on the domain of his other protegee. Hers is another long-forgotten name that I was able to recover. It is indeed incredible that her name emerged from the deep depths of my mind! Baby Pola was her stage name. Herchlikovitz who had been her patron for some time had helped to make her a star. She was a young woman refugee, probably then in her late twenties or early thirties. The songs that she sang were her specialty. I certainly could not have performed them.[10]

During those first two years in Belgium, the theater dominated your existence. What about school?

I entered the second grade of one of the branches of the *Ecole Elémentaire Communale d'Anderlecht* (District of

Anderlecht Elementary School). Girls and boys attended different schools. Both schools assimilated into their student body a number of refugee children whom I saw at various activities of the *Comité*. My teacher, Madame Didier, welcomed us into her class, three German-speaking little girls. I grew very fond of her and appreciated her encouragement to mix with the French-speaking native children, a process that took some time.

How long did it take?

Considering it now from an adult's point of view, it didn't take long at all, barely three months. In a child's mind, however, such a time span appears immense, especially when it is wrought with insecurity and embarrassing perplexities. Not knowing the language, the three of us sought comfort in each other's presence. However, we branched out as we became more fluent. Each one of us learned very quickly, and soon our vocabularies nearly equaled that of our classmates', and our pronunciation was flawless. But we didn't form new friendships with our other classmates during those first two years. The refugees had a close sense of community, and their children, because of their experience, had a quality of maturity not yet found in the local children. Perhaps there was also a feeling of inferiority, of shame, that we were so different. We had learned to communicate, but our parents as yet had not. Thus, in contrast to the native children's relationship to their parents, we became our parents' spokespeople. At times this relationship may have been flattering to a childish ego, yet it also deprived us of our comfort from parental wisdom and protection. Furthermore, as is so often the case, the victim feels shame for having been the object of persecution, so that even then, under our seeming childish unconcern, lurked the sadness at being strangers, at having had to flee.

Also, I was envious of my classmates' material comforts, especially during that first winter in our garret rooms, where the walls were so humid that icicles formed when the stove was not lit. I remember being so distressed that I mentioned my discomfort during class discussion. The next day a little girl came by to present us with a bag of coal. I didn't object to this friendly gesture, and since my parents appreciated it, I valued her parents' generosity as well. Yet it just reinforced the sadness. I had a little Belgian friend who lived with her family above her mother's and aunt's dress shop diagonally facing the *café*. Denise was not Jewish and attended a private school. Lillian, a Belgian Jewish girl, was also one of Denise's close friends. She lived on the same block, and their families socialized. The three of us often played together, but Denise was my favorite. However, I was always conscious of an inequality between us. These children's mothers took them to plays, to concerts, to matinées at the *Théâtre de la Monnaie*, the Brussels opera house. Those were privileges my family could not afford. Although I sometimes played at Denise's house, I could not reciprocate the invitation because I was ashamed of our meager living quarters. The circumstances were different with other refugee children, for we shared the experience of our temporary situation, and we visited back and forth.

The public school and the *Comité* supplied our cultural development. Of the pleasant memories of entertaining events provided by the school, one stands out especially. Usually, special events occurred in school, most often in November because of the holiday of Saint Nicholas. That first year of my public school attendance when I was in the second grade, all the pupils were taken to see Walt Disney's *Snow White*. The huge cinema was packed with children, and Mme Didier filed us row by row to our seats in the balcony. The dialogue was dubbed in French, as were the songs. I was transported; it was the most beautiful film I had ever seen. We hummed the tunes as we left the theater: *Héo, héo, nous rentrons du boulot* (hayo, it's home from work we go). Throughout my childhood years I longed to see the film again, but never did.

I also recall a particular outing, but I cannot remember who organized it. I know I was there with my refugee classmates. We were guests of the Girl Scouts; I remember their uniforms and their leaders, older teenage girls. They taught us songs and round dances, and served refreshments. One of my class-mates whose name was Herta, just like my sister, mocked the French songs because she could not pronounce or un-derstand the words. I remember ambivalent feelings about her attitude. I smiled uneasily, worrying about offending our hostesses, some of whom seemed puzzled by my friend's laughter.

Yet within a short time, all these refugee children spoke solely in French. We conversed in French among ourselves and switched to German only when speaking to our parents. French directed our daily lives; we enjoyed speaking it, so that it became our first language, and it was the medium in which we learned to express ourselves best.

Did the resentment you harbored against German enhance your quest for mastering French?

I don't know whether at the time I was aware of such a resentment. However, gaining proficiency in the new lan-guage was a natural process. Children adapt and live in the present, since they undergo constant development and inte-grate new experiences. For our parents, Belgium represented an intermediate landing. For the children, the life there had a permanency, even if only for the time being. Unfortunate-ly, later events taught the adults to resign themselves to a long stay, if not a permanent one. My dislike of the German language developed gradually as the horrors of World War II unfolded.

And Flemish? It was a compulsory subject in school.

The schoolteachers were obliged to be bilingual, and Flem-ish was taught twice weekly. Among my classmates the sub-ject produced very little interest, even among the refugee children. However, I found it amusing that Flemish was so near to German, yet so different. Perhaps I liked it because of Mme Didier's teaching method and because of my fond-ness for her. Nevertheless, my interest prevailed long after I had left her class. Although my Flemish never equaled my proficiency in French, still I progressed, and I learned to com-municate orally and in writing. Having to flee from one's native land was to become multilingual the hard way. Also, since the circumstances obliterated our childhood, we matured quickly. Yet among all the horrors that followed, I have always considered it a privilege to have grown up trilingual.

Only trilingual? You didn't include Yiddish in your inner enumeration of languages. Has your arrogance prevailed through the years?

This omission proves a point. I admit to remnants of this attitude. Nevertheless, I have throughout the years consciously tried to eradicate this disdain. But in reflecting on the past, and in considering that although I sang and spoke Yiddish learned lines in plays, the need to communicate in Yiddish was minimal at first, and nonexistent subsequently, compared with the daily usage of the other three languages. Also, it is no wonder that residues of this tendency survive because of having had our lives depend on our ability to obliterate everything that was Jewish.

So then, how exactly did the legitimate Yiddish theater enter into your life?

I don't recall the beginning - I know I never tried out. In retrospect, I can only speculate that I was seen in one of my singing performances. I found myself called upon when a child's role required casting. However, I cannot remember the name of the play; this time my memory fails me, even though I recall the story of this very successful sappy and sentimental musical. My search for information about this play, among the small scattering of old papers left to me by my parents, has yielded no results. Presumably they kept only those papers considered most important in the years of terror that followed. All else was discarded during our many moves.

Add this to your projects in search for documentation. Have we here another example of your efforts to eradicate from your mind undertakings of Jewish content in your childhood?

Of course, that is always a likely possibility. Yet another possibility may be my lack of enjoyment of the experience. There were frequent rehearsals in a drab, cold, and dusty theater; I spent long, boring periods waiting for scenes involving my role.

Didn't the applause and the success of the performance make up for the tedium?

Only my family was thrilled. For years and years my parents sang the songs featured in the play. I recall mainly the monotony and lack of comfort, especially when I had to travel with the company to the permanent residence of the theater in Antwerp. That city had the largest Yiddish-speaking community in the country and offered the most extensive programs in the Jewish arts. The job of supervisor, caregiver, and travel companion fell to my big sister Herta, then eighteen years old. We lodged in a private house. I recall the bedroom and the bathroom but have no recollection of any interaction with the family who sheltered us and who was associated in some way with the theater. The gray and rainy weather may be connected to the drab images of the permeating feelings of sadness. Herta's mood was somber too, however the reasons for her gloom may have been different from mine and beyond my knowledge.

Her mood may have influenced yours, and vice versa.

Again, I was too young to ask her about her feelings, and was conscious only of mine. I knew I was sad, but that was often a permanent condition, so it just seemed normal.

Did you worry about missing school?

I remember being concerned about it, and I was uneasy that it did not trouble my parents. My absences were certainly detrimental to my academic progress. It has occurred to me just now that Herta's lack of cheerfulness may have been connected to her ambivalence in regard to this theatrical venture, since she valued schooling very highly.

Did you enjoy the company of the other members of the cast?

די 9 יאריקע כאראקטער זינגערין
א י נ ג ע   ש ע ע ר

"The nine-year old character-singer"
On the Yiddish stage, Brussels 1939-1940.

All of them were friendly and charming, but I particularly liked the female lead. She played the role of my young governess who was in love with my widowed father. The young daughter wished and expected him to marry her governess, who would then become her legitimate mother. I especially delighted in our common song and dance number. Yet the male actors intimidated me, especially the man who played my father. I was just too young and easily influenced by moods and surroundings to appreciate the opportunity and the circumstances. I couldn't value the humor, the language, the characters, and the songs. In recalling some of the lyrics, I understand now why my family thought them so amusing. In analyzing the situation as it was then, the essential feature to consider is the additional displacement, the lack of home and familiar surroundings that added to the feelings of insecurity and uncertainty. On second thought, Herta may have been blue for the same reason.

And when you met the famous Molly Picon there, was that exciting? How did she happen to be in Antwerp?

She had just finished filming in Poland and stopped in Belgium on her way back to the United States. The cast was buzzing animatedly about her, in turn delighted and intimidated by her presence in the audience. After the performance she came backstage to greet everyone. I remember a dark-haired, gentle but discreetly ebullient woman who embraced and kissed me, saying sweet words to me in Yiddish: *Oi asoi sies* (oh so sweet), among others. It stands out as a pleasant experience because of her warmth and what I perceived then as sincerity. She seemed to behave in real life in the way that she acted in her films.

And now it appears as though a quasi-miracle occurred since your last recordings of your memoirs two days ago. It is truly a wonder that the title of that play leaped forth from your memory after you thought that it was forgotten for all time.

In truth, I was convinced of its complete oblivion - this flashback was perfectly amazing! Suddenly and unexpectedly, the recollection of an episode in my childhood and my mother's image and voice emerged, answering a question I had asked her. I had forgotten the name of the play then too, and asked her whether she could recall it. She answered, nodding nostalgically and with pride, "It was, *Mein Mame a Kaleh* " (My Mother a Bride). Thus I had forgotten that name more than once. It seems that patterns of the memory repeat themselves. The unconscious often erases experiences, especially if they are hurtful. Yet, somehow willpower may retrieve them. I know that similar patterns of veiled memories will appear on this journey into the past, and I will find them painful. I have much trepidation concerning this pursuit. I hope for strength and endurance in my commitment now to forge ahead.

A blend of sorrow and gratification emerges from that particular interval in your childhood. Yet, throughout the years, your memory carried mostly the pain.

This appears to be a pattern among child survivors. Since the sum of the experiences was so overwhelmingly negative, sadness dominates the recollection of the past. Still, one period emerges from my memory as positive, although it embodied the same components of both affliction and contentment. Logically, negative aspects should dominate the experience of "Merxplas."[11] Since its purpose was the forced internment of my father, unpleasant impressions should prevail when considering the situation rationally. Yet, pleasing recollections remain.

I recall that the Belgian authorities obliged all refugee adult men to spend several months in a camp by that name. All males of the refugee community were in turn confined to *Merxplas*. The law required provisional internment of refugees. When they had proof of future resettlement possibilities, they were set free.[12] The possibility of confinement caused considerable apprehension when my father was summoned to Merxplas. As always, my parents would not discuss it. I was told that he would leave for some time, but we would visit. That afternoon, on the eve of his departure, we went out walking, which was one of our principal means of recreation. My queries as to the cause of my parents' anxiety which was apparent in their grim expressions, were severely dismissed.

I felt guilty for not sharing their apprehension, excluded, and unworthy of an explanation. Yet again I sensed the ambivalence in the purpose of their silence. I knew that their aim was to protect me from pain.

How did Ernst avoid Merxplas?

I can only guess that he may have eluded this confinement by providing the authorities with proof of existing negotiations for his departure to South America. The *Comité* was instrumental in the procedure. As mentioned earlier, his girlfriend Rachelle's good offices there may have been influential as well.

I discovered evidence of this internment among my parents' papers. I found a tattered pass dated January 30, 1939, issued to my father by *Le Directeur des Colonies de Bienfaisance* of the *Centre des Réfugiés à la Colonie de Merxplas*, allowing him to spend the day in Brussels. Permission to leave the camp for several hours was granted for specific reasons. I recall that my father, as well as my uncle Eduard visited on occasion. For my father, the experience was at least endurable. Initially the situation was very uncomfortable, for suddenly he found he was an *inmate*. True, he was not mistreated, and the food was edible; but he had lost his freedom though innocent of any crime. However, he knew how to turn a painful episode into a productive one, thanks to his adaptability and personality. He refused to wait for his time to pass while languishing in inactivity. Instead, he organized those who were willing to participate into groups of agricultural workers. Soon they plowed the fields around the camp, then planted a variety of vegetables. The full days of physical work improved the men's mental and physical health. Of course, the authorities of the camp as well as the newly turned agricultural workers esteemed my father's leadership. He was known, was well liked, and had many friends. However, not everyone was keen to become a *farm laborer*, again a low-ranking role in middle-class Jewish values. Some men preferred dull inactivity, apart from bits of reading and writing. My uncle Eduard was one of those who disdained my father's work and leadership; I remember his imitating my father's early morning call to his fellow workers: "*Landarbeiter antreten* " (agricultural workers, make ready).

I enjoyed the general welcome of our Sunday visits. The camp was in the country, yet close enough to the city to enable us to travel by streetcar to the end of the line. We could reach our destination after a short walk. Facing the *Centre des Réfugiés*, but separated by the road and a large field, stood a massive gray structure, which was a camp for *Vagabonds* (vagrants). In the *Centre* many found comfort in the spirit of fellowship among my father's friends. In a large, bare hall filled with rows of long rectangular tables, we ate the Sunday noon meal together. I understood that the sleeping arrangements were set up in similar fashion in large halls with rows of numerous cots. I recall that the men pointed out the similarities to prison facilities, especially the iron bars on the windows. Perhaps it more closely resembled army barracks. In any case, people tried to make the best of it, and laughed and joked about their peculiar situation and their present life. In retrospect, some of that laughter may have been forced humor.

Who was at Merxplas at that time? Did Eduard's internment coincide with your father's?

Their stay at Merxplas overlapped, as did Robert's, my mother's young cousin. I recall seeing my uncle Eduard once when we visited. However, our young friend Walter's confinement corresponded with my father's, as did my cousin Max's, who appeared dejected but was cheered by our presence. We appreciated the happiness and animation engendered by our company. Many people always surrounded us. My mother, a very attractive woman, blossomed in the admiration of her beautiful voice and her large repertoire of Viennese songs. However, she didn't participate in the variety shows. She contributed in an informal manner after the noon meal, when we sat in small groups. The organized performances took place in the early evening when the dining hall was transformed into a recreation hall that included a stage and a piano.

That was the time for me to shine. Rachelle accompanied me when she came along with Ernst on our visits. However, the population of the *Centre* included several accomplished pianists, one in particular with whom I had already performed at festivities of the *Comité* . He could play every melody by ear. I presented some of my songs in Yiddish, especially my standard, *Der Chalutz*. Nevertheless, I clearly recall singing songs in Viennese dialect. Especially one, "*Marianka* " became my trademark there. It was a parody about a Czech domestic cook and her jealous lover Wenzel. The well-known Viennese *"Stiefelputzer"* (boot cleaner) was also a favorite. People greeted me by humming the melodies, or singing some of the lyrics. Even though it was never discussed, I was conscious of the effect of my performances and felt genuinely gratified to be able to bring enjoyment and relief from drudgery and boredom. Naturally, I was pleased with the atten-

The author's father's permission to leave Merxplas, in order to spend some time with his family in Brussels.

tion and my family's obvious delight in my celebrity.

I also experienced there some heartrending events that affected me deeply. One stands out in particular. On a Sunday evening a woman participant sang poignantly "*A Yiddishe Mame.*" (A Jewish Mother). As I looked about the audience, I noticed many people in tears, including several young men. It didn't matter that this wasn't a Yiddish-speaking audience, this song was familiar to everyone. It was and still is very famous and known to Jews the world over. A very young man sitting in the row behind me tried, though unsuccessfully, to muffle his sobs by pressing a handkerchief to his mouth. The man's youth, the tears, the words, and the music touched in me deep, sensitive feelings, and I felt profound pity. Scenes of painful separations flooded my imagination. Sympathy for the greatest loss in human experience, one's mother, overwhelmed me.

Did the evening end on this sad note?

What followed during that night remains in shadows; it is only this particular episode that persists in my memory. Usually an effort was made to bring the evening to a close on a cheerful note, when some of the men got onstage to sing the Merxplas theme song that was written there by a group of residents. They sang the stanzas and led the audience in the chorus.

> "In Merxplas, in Merxplas,
> ist der Himmel
> in der Nähe.
> Glücklich ist wer vergisst,
> das *Centre des Réfugiés.*"

> (In Merxplas the heavens are near,
> Happy the one who forgets
> the Center for Refugees.)

When my father returned to Brussels after about six months, Merxplas became a thing of the past. The family spoke about it only in reference to who, among our refugee acquaintances, was now scheduled to go and therefore would not be found at his Brussels domicile. Otherwise, it was an episode that had come to an end for us. Fortunately, it left me no bitterness. Also, there was little temptation for thoughts to linger, for the next event tended to erase concern over the last one. We now faced Ernst's departure for South America. Yet, this was a welcome event because he was able to escape at the brink of the outbreak of the war! He was fortunate to be among a very small number of young men who were sponsored by a Jewish agency to leave, and he seized the opportunity. He was given the guarantee only to leave Europe for Bolivia. Once there he would be totally on his own, and he was told that the conditions would be primitive. One of the big problems was lack of money. My parents had very little but provided him with practically all they possessed. Again, my mother's torment tortured me the most. Beside the pain of the separation, she was plagued by worry over his welfare. However, Ernst stoically urged my mother to bear the separation bravely, saying that he expected to be parted from us for five years. I didn't witness this exchange. At the time I was only aware of my mother's lamenting and worry over his well-being. She told me of their conversation much later, when we were in hiding and cut off from any news from him.

We probably didn't hear from him for three years, but the interval included the height of the Nazi persecution from 1942 until after the Liberation in September 1944. I knew that he left on a freighter from Marseilles. He sent letters from Strasbourg, France, which was his first stop after leaving Brussels. There he visited briefly with my father's youngest sister Rose and her husband Jacques. He also stopped in Nice, where he stayed with my father's older sister Frieda and her husband. I had never met any of my father's siblings. Rose and Jacques survived in hiding. Tragically, Frieda and her husband were deported and didn't return. By 1941, we knew that Ernst had made his way from the Bolivian capital La Paz, to Santa Cruz, and then to Cochabamba. He finally left Bolivia by smuggling himself into Argentina.

Did life change for you after his departure?

Another sadness was added. My mother's constant preoccupation and acute worry about him troubled me most. I missed him, his absence left a void. Yet, since he was a young adult and I was a child, we had lived divergent lives. My recollections of close personal interactions with him are few. Had he told me of his feelings or his hopes, I would have remembered. No doubt the same general notion among adults in terms of children's comprehension held true for him as well as for the other family members. Although deep down he had a tender nature, his outward macho values would have prevented him from breaking with this concept, had he even thought of it. He already had shown very authoritarian tendencies and was proud of his strong, and what was considered a virile personality, that brought him general admiration. Those were society's values at the time. Although often intimidated by his manner, I sensed his hidden tenderness. These notions were confirmed during my visits with him many decades later. But at the time, I was busy balancing my adjusting at school, my stage appearances, as well as my participation during festivals at the *Comité*. Of course, with Ernst's departure we no longer saw Rachelle very often, although our relationship with her father, my impresario, remained firm.

Sometime later, my parents and I moved from the attic to another furnished room on the second floor of the same house. I especially welcomed the change; the room was large and contained, to my great relief, two double iron beds painted white. I now had a bed of my own. The furniture was still dilapidated and we found the vermin problem there as well. However, this corner room was sunny and had, oh great joy, a small balcony facing the intersection of *Boulevard de la Révision* and *Rue de l'Instruction*. Herta kept a room in the attic for herself. My Aunt Pepi and cousin also moved from their garret to a room in a building on a different street close by.

Were visitors still as frequent?

Almost everyone congregated in our combination bedroom, living room, and kitchen. We still had only a small gas burner for cooking. Relatives visited frequently, among them Max and Robert, our friend Walter, and other refugee acquaintances came. People would let themselves in through the street door with a big iron key that was wrapped several times in a thick woolen sock, which we dropped to them from the balcony. Of course, we had no telephone, so people just came by unannounced, and we were always happy to see them. Conversations were lively, and since we had to provide our own entertainment, different voices often resonated, again singing old Viennese melodies. Playing card games called "rummy bridge" and "solitaire" was another pastime. This was a relatively peaceful respite. We suspected that it was only a short delay before the next ordeal. I could sense it in the mental climate around me, with the feeling of anguish lying deep in my consciousness. People spoke about the Nazi march into Czechoslovakia, into Poland. In school, and this was in the third grade, the teacher talked of war. She described the heroic resistance of the people of Finland fighting against the Red Army of the Soviet Union, which at the time was allied with Germany.

Were the Belgian children as affected as were the refugees by these accounts?

I recall their discussing the bravery of the Finns and the evil of the Germans. Yet, given their undisturbed innocence, they couldn't possibly have experienced then the same fear and the pangs of anxiety all too familiar to us. When war was declared in 1939, the Belgian children reflected their parents' optimism, saying that the Allied forces would be victorious and that they would soon defeat the Germans.

Sadly, the premonition of the next trial that just lay waiting materialized each time. With Belgium's entering the war, the greatest absurdity occurred when all Austrian and German men, being of enemy nationality whether Jewish refugees from Nazi persecution or not, had to report for internment. However, this time it meant being transported in large convoys out of the country to camps in southern France.[13]

Of course, no one knew of this situation in advance.

No, we learned it all from people who had escaped one way or another, either during the transport, or from the vile camps and who had somehow returned to Brussels.

But why did these refugees obey that call from the Belgian authorities in the first place?

The refugees concerned themselves with legality. They believed that unhappy consequences would be avoided by obedient behavior and by having papers that were in order. In retrospect, the precedent of Merxplas, which was so benign, may have been instrumental in their obedience. Many refugees who had to forfeit their nationality at the German or Austrian border were stateless and therefore were not called for internment. Usually, to be a person without a country was considered a sad condition. This time it turned out to be a blessing for my family. My father was safe and we were spared this one ordeal. However, Uncle Eduard, being married to a non-Jew had remained an Austrian and therefore was transported to an internment camp. Luckily he managed to escape and made his way back to Brussels, as did several of our acquaintances. They said that they were treated like prisoners. My uncle spoke of the horrible conditions during the transport and the dreadful situation in the camp, as well as the despicable treatment by French personnel.

Among a new group of visitors that Herta brought home was her new friend, Israel Krygier. Everyone called him "Srulek," which was either a diminutive or a nickname. This new group included a young married couple. They had all come from Poland and spoke mainly Yiddish. Although we saw them often, they mainly came to call on Herta, so she usually entertained them in her own room. My parents didn't object to Herta's budding romance with Srulek then. They assumed that this relationship was a phase in Herta's new interest in more mature friends. She was not even nineteen then, and some of these people were already in their thirties. My parents didn't interfere at the time because they didn't take it seriously. Perhaps they thought it unlikely for her to be really interested in this man Srulek, twelve years her senior. That might well have been the case if these had been ordinary circumstances and if the events that followed had not brought about another uprooting.

At Merxplas in 1939. Left to right standing are Walter Simoni, Ernst, two friends, and cousin Max Glasz. In the second row are Rachelle and the author. Seated are the author's parents.

CHAPTER III

EXODUS AND RETURN

The morning was sunny and bright on this Mother's Day of May 1940. But we heard an unusual noise, first muffled, then growing louder. Was this really the sound of cannons? Then the sirens wailed the air-raid alert! Overhead airplanes circled in the clear blue sky: German enemy planes! Presumably, said the adults, they would target bridges, railroads, and factories. Antiaircraft fire reverberated. Still not grasping the reality, we stood as if frozen on the balcony of our room, stunned by the sight of the dogfights in the sky between "our planes" and the enemy's. Soon, however, we recognized that the danger we had so desperately tried to elude had caught up with us. Radio broadcasts spread the news that German troops had overrun Holland and crossed Belgium's borders. Panic struck our hearts as we stood there on that sunny spring morning. I looked down to the street and saw Gaby, one of my Jewish classmates, walking with her father, her hand in his. Both were dressed for Sunday and carried bouquets of lilies of the valley, the traditional May flower for Mother's Day. They both looked disturbed; nevertheless, the father's face expressed determination. Oh, I said to myself, he insists on not worrying, to protect his child from care by carrying on with his planned routine. He pretends to proceed with life normally by having his little girl bring flowers home to her mother. How naive, I silently mused, soon they would have to accept reality.

Before long the frightening wail of the siren making its warning became a familiar sound. The air raids occurred day and night, adding another dimension of fear. We leaped out of bed and scrambled with the other tenants to the hideous, damp, musty cellar of the building. Most of the time the patronne of the Café was already there. I was so terrified that I dismissed thoughts of rats and other vermin and ignored the dirt floor and the nightmarish, bumpy, soot-blackened walls.

Around us the bewildered population could not comprehend how it all happened so soon, so unexpectedly. How could it be, they said that the enemy wasn't stopped at our Ligne Maginot? (Maginot Line).[14] The Belgians spoke of the cruelties that the invading German armies had inflicted on their people in World War I.

Days passed, but now people fled by the thousands, hoping to wait behind the Allied lines for the attacker to be stopped and thrown back. The streets and roads were choked with people of all ages. Entire families fled the foe; it seemed like an exodus of the whole population. People left by every possible means: in trains, automobiles, trucks, and horse-drawn carts, and of course on foot.

Once more we prepared to leave, and again with not much more than the clothes on our backs. The bit of extra we carried in small suitcases and bundles, some of which were loaded on a child's stroller. I don't think we told the patronne of our departure. But I can only speculate, since no comment was made in my presence. My parents simply locked the door of our room. Walking alongside my father who was pushing the loaded stroller, were my mother and I, followed by my Aunt Pepi and Fred, Herta and her friend Srulek, and together we joined the fleeing throng.

Why on foot, were there no trains?

I can only conjecture, since I do not recall the adults debating the matter. Under the circumstances, trains may have been terribly crowded, were probably infrequent and therefore would be unreliable. In addition, traveling in trains might have been more risky, since they were a favorite target for bombing, as were the railroad tracks. Consequently the trains might have finally stopped running altogether. It so happened that the people traveling on foot often made better progress than those in vehicles, which soon ran out of fuel and had to be abandoned. Furthermore because the roads were blocked by thousands of refugees, vehicles, could proceeded only at the same pace as the refugees on foot.

I remember hearing talk about La Panne, a resort and small port on the Belgian coast on the North Sea, as our projected destination. Another possibility was the French port of Boulogne. In any case, it was decided that we would head in the direction of the coast, and see which of the two destinations would prove more favorable. The thought was somehow to find passage across the English Channel and to escape to Great Britain, putting the sea between us and the dreaded enemy. Indeed, we were among thousands of people with the same idea. So once again we faced a new crisis. Once more we fled in search of refuge.

What recollections come to mind now as to your emotional and psychological reactions at the time?

Actually, I considered this situation just another episode in our continued refugee status. Strangely enough, I recall more vividly the feelings and emotions from earlier experiences. Later, the more stressful the conditions became, the less I remembered them, even though I was older. In a sense it was a way of coping. However, I do recall not being surprised at this new state of distress. Since we had gone from one crisis to another with sometimes shorter or longer lulls in between, I expected it to be only a matter of time before the end of the last interval and the start of a new one. Of course, I sensed tremendous urgency and danger, the fear and apprehension of this new uncertainty, but not that profound dejection that I would experience later. Perhaps at the time amid the new upheaval I still found solace in the presence of the extended family, the feeling of comfort in the common effort and involvement of each member that strengthened and renewed old bonds. As I was always sensitive to the actual mental climate around me, this condition was apt to engender confidence. That may be the reason for the scarcity of my recollection of feelings regarding this flight's onset. Certainly, in the company of one's loved ones, it is possible to surmount many trials; nevertheless I know that acute anxiety prevailed. But more significant for us was the "normalcy" of our situation at this abnormal time. For now we shared the alarm of the general population with whom we participated in an enormous upheaval, fleeing a common enemy. And to our horror, as we trudged along together on the roads, mingling with Belgian army convoys, we were periodically machine-gunned and bombarded by low-flying German aircraft.

This additional trauma remains etched in your memory. In retrospect it was naive for the fleeing civilians traveling among the military troops not to foresee these attacks.

Those roads were the ones leading to the coast. That it was civilians - men, women, and children - who constituted the majority was clearly evident. The attacking aircraft sprayed us with machine-gun fire regardless; people threw themselves into ditches by the side of the road. I recall precisely our stunned and total disbelief at this first unexpected experience. My mother, hoping to protect me with her body, flung herself on top of me.

Having already experienced fleeing, didn't you have a sense of "déjà vu," a feeling that you again walked the roads of the world in search of refuge? In your mind didn't this feeling set you apart from your fellow Belgian refugees?

Of course, I was always conscious of our own particular predicament. Nevertheless, the experience of bombardments and the proximity of actual troops engaged in war added another dimension to the feeling of terrible danger and vulnerability. Again, the fact that we felt bound to the larger population by unity and misfortune, and by a common determination, provided a positive approach to this terrible trial.

Now we did not find ourselves singled out, running from a hostile people, but instead fleeing with our allies. Under these new circumstances, the signs dotting the roads marked *"Refugiés,"* with arrows pointing in the direction for us to follow, were meant for all who sought to escape the invading foe. Similar signs directed us to stations that furnished provisions as well as shelter for the night.

Were these shelters set up in the villages' municipal buildings and schools?

I recall only halls and corridors where we bedded down on the floor on our coats, lying next to each other along the wall. One cold and drizzly evening when we first spotted such a sign, Fred and I ran ahead on the muddy road. A kind and fatherly-looking soldier directing the crowd cautioned us not to lose our families in all the commotion. I remember his words: *"ne vous perdez pas, les enfants "* (don't get lost, children). Indeed, many families were looking for their children who inadvertently had wandered off. Frightened by the prospect of anyone's straying, we always remained close together. As we trudged along the roads my mother developed terrible blisters on her feet. Since she could no longer walk, we took some of the bundles off the child's stroller, and she sat on top of it. My father pushed her until her feet healed. As the military situation deteriorated for the Allies, the shelters disappeared. Then we sought cover in farms where we slept in barns and hay-lofts. We survived on potatoes, vegetables, and milk available there. On one occasion as we left the road and walked through the fields on our way to such a farm, I was struck by how nature in full bloom reigned in its summer fecundity and provided a semblance of peace, with no sign of war. However, soon tire marks which crossed the ripening fields and flattened the growing wheat, contradicted this serenity. Also, intervals of artillery blasts shattered the seeming harmony. Observing the singing of birds, the blooming blue cornflowers and red poppies, the humming bees, the colorful butterflies fluttering in the sunshine of summer just begun, I remember contrasting this joyful scene with the anxiety in my heart. It was a rare occasion when I expressed inner feelings by voicing my astonishment to Fred as to the disparity between the moment's beauty and brief calm and the reigning turmoil in our lives. I remember his nodding in agreement.

We didn't get very far in our journey. I remember that we passed through two towns, Courtrai and Ypres in Flanders, where the houses were pitted with shrapnel marks. But then we could go no farther for we were caught in crossfire. As usual we sought refuge in a farm; luckily this one nestled in a hollow. We huddled in the barn, flattened on the ground, which rose upward and shook under the impact of the falling bombs around us. Shells from artillery guns fired low whistled past directly above our heads. We had no thought of the future, only dread of the present, each moment filled with anxiety as we feared for our lives.

During lulls in the bombardments, the farmers hurried to go on with their work in the fields. Fred and I watched the farm maids milk the cows. They were amused and flattered by our curiosity and gave us some milk. Drinking milk still warm from the cow was a new experience. It reminded us that there were peaceful, joyful, and humane things in life. As the stretches of calm grew progressively longer, news came that the enemy army had encircled us, that we were surrounded! Fearful and helpless, wondering about our fate, we awaited the outcome in the barn of that same farm. Periodic artillery fire kept moving farther into the distance as the days went by. From its sound we tried to guess which was Allied fire and which was German. We lived each hour, each moment, separately. The days had no names, no meaning. As always, my father tried to cheer everyone up with his optimism. He lessened the tension with jokes and stories about life at the farm. He attempted to instill faith in us that there would be a good outcome.

Did he invoke God? Did anyone?

I called to God fervently but silently for help and protection. The adults believed but were not pious, so traditional prayers were never recited. They prayed to God to protect our Allies and to curse the enemy. When events turned critical, they voiced their hope that "God will help." When the artillery fire and bombing stopped completely for several days, the ominous stillness presaged the imminent arrival of the enemy.

Yet, when the German soldiers finally appeared, fears were abated

The German soldiers were not vindictive as everyone had feared after hearing gruesome stories of German soldiers' atrocities during World War I. When six soldiers drove up in two armored vehicles and one motorcycle with a sidecar, the farmers and their farmhands, men and women, came out with their hands raised above their heads in surrender. Seeing this, we must have thought that it might not be a bad idea to join them, and so we did. The farmer's oldest son, acting as their spokesperson, insisted in Flemish on telling the soldiers of the farmers' noninvolvement in the fighting, and of their heritage: *we zennen Vlaams* (we are Flemish). The young Germans looked quietly amused by the scene. Wanting to win over the population, they were friendly and forthcoming. They succeeded, for the people succumbed in no time. Politely the soldiers requested shelter at the farm until their regiment was ordered to move on. The proprietors, charmed by their friendly demeanor and good looks were happy to comply with their request. The men seemed fit and in good humor, displaying no battle fatigue whatsoever. They said that the war was such an easy contest for them. Later I heard them joke among themselves recalling the hurried flight of the Allied armies as their own regiments advanced. One very blond soldier said to another that he was going to take a nap and wanted to be awakened at the proclamation of victory: *Wach mich auf nach dem Sieg* (wake me after victory). We shared the barn and hayloft with them for a very short time, perhaps a day or two. I recall seeing early one morning one of the soldiers washing at the farmyard well.

You didn't conceal the fact that you understood their language, and your parents conversed with them in German. How did they interpret this linguistic ability?

I cannot recount exactly my parents' explanation as to our presence there. I know that my father was not totally candid with them. I recall his declaring that we had fled, as had so many others, out of fear of the invading armies. The soldiers protested loudly against such apprehension. They insisted that our trepidations were for naught, that no one had reason to fear them.

Then, lacking any other alternative, we got ready to return to Brussels. In many ways we were fortunate not to have reached France, for Vichy France blocked the return of the refugees of the "exodus" and interned them in southern France in the heinous camps of Gurs, Riversaltes, du Vernet, and des Milles, from which they were ultimately shipped to the assembly camp of Drancy near Paris, and on to the death camps.[15] When we started to walk back, the Germans by then had completely occupied the country, all the way to the coast. I recollect some images that left sad impressions along this journey, such as the graves of Allied and German soldiers by the side of the road. The helmets of the fallen soldiers hung from the crosses marking the burial place. We paused each time we passed a site identified by an Allied helmet; my mother would say *"nebich"* (a Yiddish word used universally, meaning "poor one, such mischance, such a pity"), and I would echo her words. Another vivid, enduring memory of our returning journey was of the somber streams of Allied prisoners on country roads and in villages. Dejected, tired, and dirty, they formed a heartbreaking picture. My aunt Pepi and Fred told of seeing a French officer begging for water from a villager who was standing by, observing the humiliating scene. Deeply saddened and depressed, we continued on our way.

Did you now in turn endure Allied artillery fire and bombardments?

All noticeable Allied combat and resistance had stopped, their troops in retreat, in disarray, or taken as prisoners.

At least there was relief from this one frightful danger. But then wasn't it surprising that except for once, you never encountered any other Jewish refugees?

Although bombardments and cannon fire were horrible and terrifying, we would have welcomed them on the part of the Allies. It would have inspired hope, announced their resistance and denied their surrender. Years later when Allied planes appeared, we ran out into the street cheering wildly in spite of the possible danger of bombs. As to other Jewish refugees, some may have been Jewish but unknown to us. I cannot say why we didn't meet more. Perhaps they disappeared among the throngs because of their small numbers. Possibly, some of them used more comfortable means of transportation. The adults never discussed the subject in my presence. I never thought of it until now. However, as we journeyed back, we encountered one Jewish family. We recognized them at once by the special demeanor and dress of the four adults and two small children. All were small and slight in stature, and their clothes announced their religious piety. The warm weather notwithstanding, the men wore black city suits and felt hats. The women's long-sleeved dresses fell to their mid-calves, and kerchiefs covered their heads. They had stopped to rest in the shade, sitting on a low wall to feed the children. We stopped, and the adults exchanged a few words. They spoke Yiddish and remarked to each other, motioning in our direction, *"se zennen Yidden"* (they are Jews). They also may not have met many other Jews. They said that they had originally come to Belgium from Poland, had lived in Antwerp and then fled, and now were turning back as well.

How long had you been away after you finally arrived at your former living quarters?

I can only guess, about four to six weeks. The summer school vacation had not ended. My gentile Belgian friend Denise, who lived diagonally across from our building, saw me on our balcony. She waved and motioned to come down to play. She asked where we had been during the past weeks, for she had noticed our absence and had missed me. I found it surprising that she and her family had not attempted to flee as well. But soon I dismissed the thought, surmising that after all, my friend's family did not have the same motives as our own. Besides, we were back where we started, so their decision had been wise. As all who had stayed home, they had spared themselves many dangers and much discomfort.

And so we coped as best we could. Of course, the *Comité* had disappeared along with its support and sociability. Gone as well were public Jewish performances. We tried our best to ignore the German presence, but in time it became harder to do. At first, mostly the German soldiers were in evidence. Nevertheless, everyone knew of the establishment of the *Gestapo*[16] with its headquarters on *Avenue Louise* in the most fashionable district of the city. We felt its threatening presence even while they held their operations in abeyance for the time being.

For about a year and a half, the Jews of Belgium adjusted to the new political reality with the rest of the population. When school resumed, I entered the fourth grade. Some of the refugee children I had known before the invasion had moved, but many also returned to the same school. Life took on a semblance of normalcy; people adapted and tried to ignore the widespread presence of German troops. The entire cabinet of the Belgian government had fled to London. However, King Leopold III opted, as he said, to "remain with his people." He capitulated to the Germans. Elisabeth, the queen mother, remained as well. She was to play an important role in saving Jewish children during the terrible years that lay ahead.

Were you at that time familiar with these political concerns? Did children your age discuss these matters?

As always, I listened carefully to adult discussions. Also, schoolchildren argued heatedly about whether the King should have fled or remained, abdicated, and so on, their views depending on their own families' outlook. Arguments often arose in the *vestiaire*, a small peg-lined cloakroom adjacent to each classroom. In my fourth grade, pro and con discussions would often take on passionate proportions. The opposing view accused the apologists for the King of being cooperators with the enemy. Finally, the teacher, disturbed by the excited voices, forbade discussion of the subject in school. In that same cloakroom, my fellow refugee children and I, known for our knowledge of the German language, were occasionally accused by our classmates of being *Boches*, a French derogatory slang expression meaning Germans. On the other hand, we were at times also called *Smous*, an insulting Flemish anti-Semitic epithet. Children often threw these remarks at us when irritated at us or jealous for various reasons. We learned to dismiss them, seeing the irrationality. On the one hand we were *Boches* because we came from German-speaking countries, on the other we were *Smous* because we fled from persecution. We laughed at being called Germans, but we only suppressed the hurt of the insulting expression for Jew. Jews were generally disliked and mistrusted. On occasion when discussions of religious customs arose, the phrase *votre Dieu, c'est un faux* (your God is a fake) was contemptuously expressed by some of our gentile classmates. The teacher never interfered in the latter arguments, nor did she forbid name-calling.

She may not have been aware of the name-calling. After all, you never complained to her.

True, and these arguments may not have been as loud as the previous ones. However, it never occurred to us to speak to her, mainly because we thought it useless. We always sensed that she harbored anti-Semitic feelings, though not strong ones - but that she was prejudiced nevertheless. We suspected that she didn't halt the arguments because she was rather amused by them and silently approved.

You never spoke of the children's anti-Semitic expressions among your Jewish classmates. However, you discussed the teacher's remarks.

We believed the children's attitude not worth discussing. As for the teacher, we didn't worry terribly about her. We acknowledged sadly but realistically some latent anti-Semitism as a norm among the general population. On occasion, the Jewish children, both Belgians and refugees, talked about one of the outspoken and bold Jewish girls. Having had to repeat some grades, she was two years older but still in the fourth grade. This girl held her own when replying to the teacher's veiled remarks. Of course, I never spoke of the situation at home for questions were rarely posed regarding school. Had I been asked, I would have mentioned it. I didn't actively dislike the teacher; I only felt an incompatibility with her teaching and personality. For the first time in my years at school, my work was poor. Had I discussed this with an intelligent and sensitive adult, many suppressed problems could have surfaced, been explained, and perhaps resolved.

And Herta? She certainly was sensitive and intelligent.

True, but she was also young and inexperienced. Besides, she was unfamiliar with the development of the situation as well as the potential psychological consequences. By then, matters had become complex and needed untangling. She didn't know how to question me, and knew only that I was unhappy and worried. Also, with no experience in children's psychological development and motives, she was unprepared, in spite of all her good will, to engage the teacher to seek possible solutions. Nevertheless, I did finally voice my concern, and Herta agreed to speak to the teacher, since neither of my parents felt that their knowledge of French was adequate for in-depth discussion.

Herta made no appointment; that may have been the reason the interview was so very casual. It took place in the school courtyard during recess. The teacher was soon on the defensive and presented a litany of examples of my poor performance. Herta's inexperience quickly became apparent. Unable to draw out any information from the teacher, she was overcome by emotion, her voice trembling, and was on the verge of tears.

I wound up feeling humiliated, sorry for my sister and guilty for having caused her embarrassment. I knew her tender heart and felt that she believed that she had failed. Yet, her opinion regarding the teacher's obtuseness notwithstanding, I instinctively accepted once and for all the obligation to rely solely on myself in the future.

But you were only ten years old.

Of course I was very insecure and nervous. When making decisions of any kind, I depended mostly on my intuition. I think that some rational thought process was probably involved as well, only I was not aware of my own analyzing.

This encounter with your teacher occurred after Herta's marriage?

I think so. Herta got married shortly after our return when we still lived on the corner of *rue de l'Instruction* and *boulevard de la Révision.* My parents disapproved of her choice; they felt that at age nineteen, she was too young and that her husband-to-be, twelve years her senior, was too old for her. In addition, he had no particular profession or trade skill. They thought so even when we were fleeing Brussels.

Left to right are Herta, the author's mother, Aunt Pepi and cousin Fred. In front is the author. Brussels, 1941.

Was it wrong of them to let him join us, seeming to integrate him into the family? Perhaps they realized this in retrospect. However, at the time of our flight, my parents' position was untenable because of the pressure of the circumstances. Casting him out would have seemed morally wrong. Because he had no family, they felt obliged to accept his company. Besides, the pressing situation had left no time for deliberations. Nevertheless, after sharing hardships and dangers so intimately, it was perhaps naive on their part to expect the relationship to break up. They hoped that given their opposition, Herta would listen to them. In addition, their legal consent was required, since she was under the age of twenty-one. Of course she knew of their resistance, yet she arranged all the legal particulars for the marriage to take place.

The morning of the ceremony at the *Maison Communale,* the City Hall, my mother refused to get out of bed. I can still see the room, with Herta's tugging at my mother, imploring her to get up because her presence was compulsory. Poor

Herta and Srulek in their wedding picture. Brussels, 1941.

Herta, so attached and devoted, how difficult and sad this disagreement must have been for her. Ultimately my mother yielded and we all went to the *Maison Communale*. Religious ceremonies were optional and always separate from the compulsory civilian one where the actual marriage was recorded. We waited in the back of a large hall, watching the completion of a preceding marriage. My Aunt Pepi sat between Fred and me, my parents in front of us next to Herta and her husband-to-be. My aunt critically pointed out to me the groom's neckline and his need for a haircut. Since two witnesses were required for each partner, some of his friends must also have been present, most likely the young couple that had often visited Herta. I have a strong sense of their being there, but no actual visual recollection of their attendance.

Was this union celebrated in any way after the return from City Hall?

Again, no visual recollection comes to mind, only the sense of a small afternoon gathering in our room for modest refreshments and coffee.

How can you be sure of this event if you cannot actually remember it? Isn't it because it seems most likely that such a humble celebration took place ?

True, I can't be certain, since I don't recall any particular instances or conversations, and it makes sense to think that some sort of gathering was in order after a marriage ceremony. Again, I can only emphasize this strong impression.

In any case, notwithstanding all the misgivings concerning this marriage, her husband Srulek was ultimately accepted. However, my parents' opinion that she was too good for him endured. The couple set up housekeeping in two small rooms on *Rue de France* near the *Gare du Midi* in the district of *St.-Gilles*, a fifteen-minute walk from us. Just like our building, theirs also housed a *brasserie* on the ground floor, and the *patron* of that *café* served as manager of the building as well. However, he didn't intimidate me as did the *patronne* of the *brasserie* where we lived. He was jovial and friendly, as was his wife. His kindness as well as the goodness and cordiality of some of the other tenants would prove to be greatly comforting in the difficult time that lay ahead.

Assertiveness was often required in my frequent role as spokesperson for my parents, whose French was still limited. The recent circumstances had made me much older in just one year. I had matured greatly and was not easily intimidated.

Yet your father managed well in Flemish.

He had more affinity for Flemish because of its similarity to German. French required more effort for him. Nevertheless, he never really tried actually to master the language; when he spoke Flemish, it was often riddled with distorted German. The general emphasis was on getting by. However, his good nature when making himself understood charmed his listener, who forgave him his errors. Most of the people to be dealt with spoke French, and there I acted as the main spokesperson. But he managed adequately for his living. Of course, the middlemen who provided him with orders for his work were mostly Jews who spoke Yiddish.

Soon after Herta's marriage, we moved to larger quarters, about one block around the corner on *Rue de l'Instruction*. We lived in three rooms on the ground floor of a house that held three apartments, one on each floor. Madame Gaby, as we called her by her first name, lived on the second floor with her husband. She served in a managerial capacity, mainly in collecting the rent for the landlord. A woman in her early fifties, she originally came from Poland and kept her Jewish identity a secret. Except for our family, no one in the neighborhood knew that she was Jewish including her elderly Belgian spouse. They had just married after having lived together for several years. She wanted to shield herself from persecution by assuming her husband's Belgian nationality through marriage and hoped that her identity would never be questioned. Our family was her emotional outlet and support. She often confided her sentiments to my parents in Yiddish. In addition, she frequently reminded me never to tell anyone that she was *a Yiddishes kind* (a Jewish child), and I swore to secrecy each time.

On the third floor lived Madame Yvonne, a Flemish woman in her early thirties, with her three young children, she too was called by her first name. Her husband had volunteered for work in Germany but returned on leave about three times a year. On those occasions the children often spoke of the many goods that their father brought with him from Germany, such as nice face soap, and canned meats and fish, items that had disappeared from the shops in Brussels. The father unwrapped some of these goods in my presence once when I was playing with the children in their apartment. The family conversed in Flemish, yet they were all bilingual. Madame Yvonne was kind and jovial, but of questionable morals. It was said that when her husband was away and she could not pay the rent, she would replace the payment with her personal favors to the landlord. This behavior was confirmed for me one day when Madame Yvonne had paid us a visit and the landlord - an elderly lecher - came looking for her and urged her to lead him to her apartment on the pretense that he had to inspect its condition. He kept repeating: *mais, venez Madame Yvonne, venez!* (but come along, Mme Yvonne, come along!). Madame Yvonne tried to put off leaving, but found no other way but to relent. She finally left, and he eagerly followed. Also, in her husband's absence she had frequent visits from her lover Fritz, a tall red-haired German soldier for whom she had great affection. She often told me, how good Fritz was to her in contrast to her violent husband, who frequently beat her as well as the children. Sometimes the oldest girl confided in me about the family's problems. One night when their mother was out and the children were alone, the father returned unexpectedly. All three were petrified with fear, and when he inquired as to their mother's whereabouts, the smallest one, a boy of about four, answered in tears, "She is with Fritz." The two older girls found this amusing for reasons I never understood.

A large basement room served as my father's workshop for cutting, assembling, and sewing rabbit pelts as linings for coats and jackets. The result of breathing in the loose rabbit hair contributed to his health problems years later, first with asthma and then with emphysema. On one of the visits from that same lecherous landlord, to collect the rent from Madame Gaby and to inspect the building, he asked to see this workshop. Perhaps it was on a Sunday, since no one was working and the room was locked. In my role as spokesperson for the family, I took the key and he followed me down the basement stairs. As I unlocked the door, I felt him pressing himself against me, with his hands moving on my hips. Instinctively alert, frightened, and disgusted, I pushed the door open, slipped by him, and ran upstairs.

I didn't keep this particular incident to myself - I spoke of it immediately to my mother. However, the landlord was never confronted; probably because of our vulnerable position and our fear of reprisal. The only precaution taken was that an adult would always be with me in the presence of this man.

I couldn't have predicted the fact that my parents' need for me to act as their spokesperson, which prevented them from hiding me apart from themselves in the terrible years that followed, preserved my sense of normalcy and equilibrium in adulthood. My fellow former hidden children often voice surprise upon learning that my parents and I stayed hidden together. It is ironic that although I was robbed of my childhood during those terrible years, my parents' need for me prevented my being psychologically damaged by separation, as were so many hidden children whose parents, for their children's safety, agreed to separate. The language problem was only the initial motive for my parents' reliance on my ability and my subsequent unconscious internalization of my acceptance of that responsibility. Unbeknown to us all (and explained later in the book), what lay ahead at the time were Herta's words addressed in a letter to me at age twelve.

Those words broadened my obligation to my parents, which I carried from then on for the rest of their lives.

People listened clandestinely to the BBC for news of the war. Gloomily we heard that Hitler's armies were still defeating the Allies. Nevertheless, talk of hope persisted; with patience and endurance, sooner or late, we would see the enemy beaten. For about a year and a half, until the middle of 1941, Jews carried on with their lives as did the rest of the Belgian population. The primary everyday concern was to obtain proper food and clothing. In school we were given extra milk rations. Every day during recess milk was ladled from a large metal container into our white ceramic bowls by the teachers on duty in the schoolyard. I can still picture Mme Libert, my fourth grade teacher, a very slight woman, at what seemed a fairly strenuous task. Often when the large container was almost empty it had to be leaned to the side to fill the ladle. Because the milk tasted sweet and warm, rumors spread that it was canned and condensed and therefore diluted with warm water.

Do you have any happy memories of that time?

No, I can only recall periods free of unhappiness; I felt mostly boredom and loneliness and often the recurring feeling of foreboding. My parents' communications with me centered exclusively around physical needs. Both of them worked with furs. My mother who had never trained in any particular skill, enjoyed helping out as best she could in my father's workshop. My friendships with some of my classmates were amicable, yet lacked depth. The loneliest period was summertime, for none of my classmates participated in the day camp *Colonie Neerpede* for elementary school-children which was run by the local city government services. We would ride by chartered streetcar to an enclave outside the city. In its center surrounded by sand, lay a man-made small pond, round and shallow. The fountain in the middle was occasionally turned on. I recall no organized activity; the children amused themselves on their own. The older ones organized talent shows, and the younger ones made sand castles and competed in making different shapes of mud pies decorated with designs from colored chalk and pebbles. We carried our own lunch.

Despite my performing background, I didn't participate in the talent shows, but not because of any sense of superiority. I thought that I had nothing to offer that would be appreciated. I envied my cousin Sonia, with whom I wished I were on speaking terms but wasn't, probably because at the time our families were estranged as a result of some argument between Sonia's mother and Aunt Pepi and my mother. One afternoon I noticed a cluster of admiring youngsters around Sonia who was demonstrating how she danced on her toes, accompanying herself by singing a marching song. I remember announcing: *c'est ma cousine* (this is my cousin), and no one's paying any attention to me. Most of the time I tried to kill time, waiting for the end of the afternoon and the trip back to the city. Yet, I expected to be just as bored for the remainder of the day. My feelings of neglect contributed largely to my sadness. Many parents awaited their children at the streetcar stop when they returned. Of course, I was able to return home on my own since the final stop was so close by and I had walked that way many times. Nevertheless, I complained to my mother and insisted that she meet me too. I convinced her, for she was often there when the streetcar arrived. Sometimes she met me when I was already on my way home, smiling sheepishly for being late. How trivial this sadness appeared later compared with the heartbreaking pain we were soon to experience.

CHAPTER IV

PERSECUTION & DEPORTATION

When classes resumed in the fall of 1941, I returned to school. However, all Jewish children were very aware of the civil rights restrictions that Jews had started to face. We heard the adults discuss how Jewish teachers, professors, physicians, and lawyers were being fired from their positions. By then we also knew that all Jewish businesses, as well as all individual Jews, were ordered to record themselves in a special Jewish register. One by one, decrees by the German occupier were put in place so that within several months, Jews found themselves totally isolated from the rest of the population. By June 1942 all Jews, including children from age two on had to wear the yellow star. The following month, in July, all Jews' identity cards had a red stamp attesting *Juif /Jood* ("Jew" in French and Flemish). Jews were barred from all public institutions, such as museums, libraries, sporting events, concerts, theaters, cinemas, and swimming pools. Also, Jews had to observe a special curfew that required them to be indoors by 8 P.M. As the year progressed, we heard that Jewish physicians, fired from hospitals and clinics, could treat Jewish patients only privately, and that gentile doctors were forbidden to treat Jews. In addition, Jews could reside only in certain cities, were forbidden to live in the countryside or to leave the country, and that in the coming school year Jewish children would be barred from public schools.[17]

Always in fear and threatened with more trouble and re-percussions, Jewish people abided by the orders imposed on them. Jews were always careful to be within the law, hoping that no other restriction would follow. Thus the enemy spun a careful web of psychological preparations in planning its goal. After each circumvention, the Germans waited before issuing the next restriction. With people in compliance and with no reactions from the Belgian authorities or other governments, the Germans stealthily decreed one by one ever more restraining laws. Each time they waited, and meeting no consequences, continued until Jews were totally defenseless and trapped.

At the start of June 1942, a large number of Jewish young men were summoned for obligatory work in northern France to build the Atlantic fortification wall under the supervision of the German organization Todt. The feeling of anguish in the Jewish community grew perceptibly. However, the Germans camouflaged this requisition for obligatory work by persuading the Belgian authorities to cooperate; insisting that this endeavor would reduce the number of unemployed workers in the country. The Belgians complied and called up each "worker" individually. Since only the unemployed were qualified, they examined carefully each worker's means of subsistence, and then each one was given a physical exam. All of this disguise gave the operation the semblance of reliability, thus fooling the people into believing that this was a legitimate plan of work. The Germans stayed in the background, and came forth only after the Jews, responding to the call by the Belgians, presented themselves.[18]

Foolishly, Herta's husband Srulek answered such a summons. Not seeing any viable alternative as an unemployed Jewish man, he responded, afraid of otherwise being hounded, caught, severely punished, and deported to a much worse fate. And like all those who obeyed, he was naive. People refused to give up hope and wanted to trust in what they were told. They resigned themselves to the idea that they must do compulsory work for the German war effort and that they had no alternative but to obey. So, like so many hundreds of young men, Srulek thought in this way and therefore he left.[19]

Herta was very unhappy, of course. We were all stunned by the event but had no resources for other options. We saw no other choice. Ultimately my sister was very stoic about it. Some unemployed Belgians had already volunteered for work in Germany, so that people drew parallels and believed that even though Jews did not volunteer, work was the aim of the plan.

Shortly after Srulek's departure, panic struck again in the Jewish community when more people were summoned for obligatory work. They were ordered to present themselves at *Caserne Dossin*, a former fort in the city of Malines, later used by the Belgians as army barracks. There the Jews would be assembled to be transported for work in countries to the east. Anyone resisting was threatened with repercussions not only to himself but also to his family, his relatives, and ultimately the whole Jewish community. Indeed, that threat was written on the summons. To execute this plan, the Germans had formed by the end of 1941 a Jewish bureaucracy named *AJB* for *Association Juive de Belgique*.[20] This agency held a complete registry of all Jews living in Belgium and employed four thousand Jews, some of whom hand-delivered the summons to thousands. Those employed by the *AJB* were protected, that is, for the time being they were sheltered from deportation.

I clearly recall the time when my then seventeen-year old cousin Fred was called. He was smiling as he announced the news; his best friends were going too, and he was delighted. He thought of it as an adventure with many other young people, a change from an uninteresting existence. Aunt Pepi was beside herself, devastated that he would welcome such a summons. She urged my parents to persuade him to resist, to hide him, in a word, *to do something*. How could anyone know what to do, my brother-in-law had gone already! My mother was frantic. Without resources, where could they hide him, and wouldn't it be worse for him and for the rest of us if he were caught? Bewildered, my parents couldn't offer an alternative.[21]

In retrospect, it could have been that Fred foolishly and perhaps subconsciously saw this as a way to free himself from his poor mother; after all, at age seventeen he was old enough to have devised his own way to resist and hide. But as far as I could see, he never considered resisting and hiding on his own, and neither did any of his friends. Perhaps he expected an experience similar to Merxplas, the benign work camp where my father had been interned in 1938 by the Belgian authorities. How was anyone to know, how could anyone fathom the enemy's murderous schemes?

Accustomed to having her family come to her rescue, my aunt would not forgive my parents; in her mind they had not done enough to stop him. They should have done something, anything, though she didn't know or tell them what they should do. After Fred left she stayed away and stopped speaking to us. We were injured, totally bewildered, helpless, and devastated. I remember seeing her last through the open door of a grocery store, when I was with my mother. My aunt was speaking to someone beside her while looking at us, saying loudly that unlike my mother who had not assisted her son Fred, she herself had once helped to watch my hospitalized sister, referring to a very difficult time, before the use of penicillin, when at age thirteen in Vienna, Herta had been gravely ill with an ear infection before a mastoid operation. In other words, my aunt meant that she had watched over Herta but that my mother had not watched over Fred. In a word, had my mother done her duty, Fred would still be with her.

Sadly, those were Aunt Pepi's feelings; in such pain, she was irrational. I recall my support for my parents as would any child, and my sense of outrage at the injustice of her accusations. Remembering this episode many years later, I realized the torture that my poor aunt must have endured, and my mother's anguish for her as well as her torment at her sister's accusations.

Did anyone attempt a reconciliation?

I was not aware of any. I believe my parents thought it useless for the time being; they expected rejection and were hurt by her allegations. During the separation from her in the ensuing months, there were many dreadful events that overwhelmed us as they followed one after the other in quick succession.

And Herta, didn't she try to speak to Aunt Pepi?

I don't know. I never witnessed any such discussions. I was deeply disturbed at the time by this tragic quarrel and have always recalled it. I remember all the conversations on the subject that were held in my presence. My sister may have been just as hurt; after all, lacking an alternative, she had resigned herself to let her husband go. Most likely she also thought my aunt irrational and unjust. Poor Pepi, it was the first time in my memory that she was not with us. Her pain and my mother's pain must have been unbearable. We carried on as best we could each day, our hearts heavy with grief and insecurity.

To alleviate her depression and loneliness after her husband's departure, Herta suggested to my parents that I stay with her. My company was of comfort to her; we had always enjoyed each other and I welcomed the change. I also appreciated being able to communicate in French. Although Herta still had a slight accent, she spoke French fluently. My parents had not mastered the language, and I continued speaking German with them. This increased our predicament. Since we were fearful of the potential consequences of appearing foreign, we were mostly silent outdoors; at best we communicated only in whispers. Given all the difficult circumstances, when with Herta I welcomed the respite of not having to cope with this language stress.

Of course you couldn't have been aware then of the reason for your feelings of relief.

Perhaps not consciously, but I think these sentiments would have come to the fore had anyone raised the subject with me. Besides, although Herta was an adult and a young married woman and I a child, our conversing in the language we came to love proved that not only did we share memories of the past, but also that we had integrated the present in our lives, and language was an important part of that process.

Yet I was lonely. I spent my time primarily among adults. Most of my former friends had moved, and I was cut off from the children in my old neighborhood. Still, in all our moving about I had formed no strong attachment with my former friends, therefore I didn't miss them as people. On the other hand, although I was happy with my sister, I craved the company of other children and went searching for them. I noticed some nearby, older boys and girls as well as someone's brother and sister my age. I met them and found that they all lived in adjacent buildings, but that none were Jewish. It was summertime, and so we lingered in the street in the evening. This was after Jews were already restricted to the eight o'clock curfew. Herta, who was always cautious not to break any laws, didn't object, since I was not far from the building's front door. I had little in common with these children other than our age and the wish to play. I had little affinity with the girl my age, but I remember best the four-teen-year-old Andrée then at the dawn of womanhood. I was intrigued by her interest in flirting with boys. Flattered by my attention and curiosity, she took me under her wing. This was not only a first exposure to a new level in social interaction, but also my apprenticeship in hiding my true identity; and in order to do so, I lied and invented stories. I could hide my background there where no one knew me. I didn't have to explain my parents' inability to converse in French, because no one ever saw them. Also, my new friends hardly ever spoke with my sister and when they did, they never inquired about her slight accent.

When confronted with a troublesome situation or question, I came up with explanations on the spur of the mo-

ment. One morning Andrée and I encountered Herta returning from an agency, perhaps the *Association Juive de
Belgique (A.J.B.)* where she may have gone hoping to find
news of her husband's whereabouts; she was always running
to various agencies, trying to get news. I remember smiling
at our encounter; I was always proud of her good looks and
her stylish appearance, and was pleased at having Andrée
meet her for the first time. However, I was taken aback by
Herta's worried look and accusing tone of voice, but I don't
recall what she disapproved of in my behavior or actions.
Herta was obviously unhappy because her efforts had once
more been in vain, and her mood probably had nothing to
do with me. After my sister went off in the opposite direction and my friend and I continued our walk, Andrée asked
me whether my sister was Jewish: *ta soeur est juive?* Astounded
I asked what made her think so. Andrée had noticed my
sister's yellow star on her blouse. I had completely forgotten
Herta's wearing it. A quick explanation was in order. I said
that my sister's husband was Jewish, that he had been sent
away for compulsory labor, and that she was inquiring as to
his whereabouts. Also, since wives automatically acquire their
husband's nationality, my sister also became Jewish. But she
was not really Jewish, only married to a Jew. Andrée nodded, seemingly satisfied with the explanation.

And then there was the time when I went with Andrée to a
swimming pool (forbidden to Jews) that required a long streetcar ride. We stayed too late and were still en route back at
8:30 in the evening. I feared that Herta would be anxious,
but I also fretted about staying out after the eight o'clock
curfew. I worried that my great apprehension might arouse
my new friend's suspicion. She was clearly surprised and
annoyed at the fuss I made about my sister's concern. The
matter of the curfew for Jews had never come up and I doubt
that she was aware of it. I was worried because Herta obeyed
it and I knew she wanted me home.

My relationship with these children halted abruptly after a
dialogue with one of the boys. This was also the first time I

knew that I had been found out. Clément, one of the young teenage boys had a German friend whose father was involved in some commercial endeavor in Brussels. There was gossip in the group that members of Clément's family were German sympathizers and considered suspicious. In any case, this German boy sometimes joined with Clément in the gathering of children at the front door of one of the buildings in the evening. His being there made us uncomfortable at first, but he was witty, amicable, and fairly handsome. Besides, no one dared to object to his presence. That was when I made my first big mistake. I carelessly let on that I spoke German, whereupon he immediately engaged me in German conversation and continued to do so at subsequent encounters.

You buried your head in the sand, thinking that you could fool everyone.

This was my apprenticeship; I was still naive, and a careless liar. One evening this boy said to me in German: "why don't you tell the truth about yourself. . .?" and some more words in the same vein. The minute my answer was out, I knew that it was wrong. My reaction was typical of someone caught lying. I jumped up, replied angrily to the accusation of not telling the truth, and left in a huff, followed by his knowledgeable grin that remained indelible in my mind. Later I reproached myself for my impulsive reaction. Had I been this careless a year later when the situation for Jews had deteriorated even more, such a mistake could have been disastrous. I integrated the experience subconsciously and learned how to proceed should a similar situation occur. Little did I know then how much this instruction would be needed in the future during the continuous hiding of my identity.

After this incident, very soon life for Jews became increasingly difficult. When people ceased to respond to the summons, the Germans started daily roundups. At the spur of the moment busy intersections in the city were cordoned off as the Germans went in search of Jews. They demanded identification, and those unlucky individuals caught in their trap were carted off to the Gestapo headquarters and from there to the assembly camp of Malines to be deported in the next convoy. Jews then ventured outdoors as little as possible, especially during the day, and the Germans began roundups at night, going from house to house in Jewish neighborhoods. That was when, in our search for safety, we started spending the night in a clothing factory for German uniforms.

Was this factory run by Belgian collaborators?

I heard the adults say that it had been requisitioned by the Germans and that the owners had been ordered to make uniforms. Some of the adults expressed doubt as to whether the owners had resisted this order. In any case, given the product manufactured there, it was considered an unlikely place for the Germans to come searching for Jews. Soon we remained there during the day as well. We shared this first hiding place with a small number of other Jewish families, and for some time none of us went out. Families sent out the children with the thought that they were less conspicuous. I would line up at grocery stores for basic foods or buy whatever was available. All of us were vigilant not to be followed. Before returning, I would pass the front door of the factory and go at least once around the block, always alert, making certain no one was tracking me.

When people remained inside the factory during the day, some of them worked there. I saw the women sew on uniform buttons, and the men did various chores such as maintenance and cleaning. Those with some tailoring ability were cutting the material. I recall being in the workshop and sewing on buttons too, but I don't recall other children's being there. In the evening we hung around in the courtyard. But our relationship with the other families remained distant. I have little recollection of them, except of one distinguished middle-aged German Jewish couple and their bespectacled daughter, a girl of about seventeen whose ambition was to become a teacher. She sat for days on end reading a big dictionary. When I questioned her as to her reasons for this, she replied that she hoped to keep up in this way with her education. I remember being impressed with her intellectual tenacity.

How did you find out that a night roundup had taken place in your neighborhood?

When someone risked returning quickly to our apartment to collect some items to make our stay in the factory more bearable, Mme Gaby, the Jewess incognito, told the story. One night she heard the sounds of motor vehicles and the slamming of car doors; these were ominous signs, given that practically all private cars and trucks had been requisitioned by the Germans, and that everyone knew of the night raids. She soon realized that a roundup was in progress. However, that night Mme Gaby succeeded in deceiving the Germans; they believed she and her husband were an elderly Belgian gentile couple. Mme Gaby congratulated herself for having married her former *bon ami;* that night she avoided being carted off with the many Jewish men, women, and children of the neighborhood. I heard her tale a short time later as she recounted her feelings of terror manifested by violent stomach cramps at the sound of those foreboding signals coming from the street. She was to experience those dread-arousing noises again, as were we. But first came the devastating report that threw the family into deep depression. The Germans had raided several blocks of the neighborhood, and Aunt Pepi was among those carted off that night. My family was numb, words failed everyone, and we were in deep anguish. My parents' distress was extreme. My mother was senseless with shock. Sometimes my mother voiced her despair, but she most often internalized her pain. On occasion she said that she had no more tears left. Therefore when she did cry, it was all that much more ravaging for me.

How did you find out about Pepi?

I can't recall exactly who risked a visit to my aunt's room and spoke to her landlady, who lived on the ground floor of the building; it may have been my uncle Eduard. I remember certain details discussed in my presence: the landlady had said that after the Germans entered the building, she stayed in the hallway and stood at the bottom of the stairs when my aunt came down, followed by a German. Concealing her gold watch in her hand, Pepi attempted to leave it in the landlady's palm as she shook the woman's hand. However, the German noticed the procedure and confiscated the watch. Pepi had hardly anything of value except that gold watch familiar to all of us, which she treasured. The Germans sealed her room, just as they sealed every residence belonging to the Jews they caught and arrested.

Did your parents attempt to discover her whereabouts?

All arrested Jews were taken to the assembly camp at the *caserne Dossin* in the town of Malines, then simply referred to by the dreaded word of *Malines*. It was from there that Pepi, with all the other Jews who were caught that night,

Aunt Pepi, Brussels 1940.

was deported with the next convoy to the concentration camps in eastern Europe. We never heard from my aunt again.[22]

How naive it was for your family to leave your hiding place at the factory and return to the apartment.

That is easy to say in retrospect. Everyone reasoned that the neighborhood, having already been raided, would now be safe. No doubt the Germans anticipated this assumption for they raided again and trapped more Jews who had eluded them the first time.

Still, foolishly we returned, and Herta went back to her own place on rue de France, a street mixed with industrial and residential dwellings where not many Jews were believed to reside. That may have been the reason this street was not included in the roundup for it lay outside our immediate district known as "a Jewish neighborhood." One day Mme Yvonne, the tenant on our third floor, said to me: "Herta better watch out, the Germans most probably will soon come to rue de France." When I repeated her words to my parents and sister, they urged me to question Mme Yvonne further. How did she know this ? Her liaison with the German soldier aroused suspicion. Did *he* communicate this information to her ? Intuitively I felt that Mme Yvonne simply conjectured on her own that the immediate neighboring district might be raided next. Yet at my parents' urging I prodded her for more information. My instincts proved correct; she really knew nothing. She spoke merely out of concern and was quite incensed to hear that we suspected her to be close to some source. She asserted over and again that her German lover Fritz was merely in the army, a plain soldier totally removed from any aspect connected with arrests or persecutions of Jews, Resistance Fighters, or anyone else. Ultimately we accepted her explanation, Herta stayed in her own small quarters and I remained with my parents.

How did your uncle Eduard - your mother's brother reappear in the picture ?

One day he simply showed up all by himself. He said he chose to leave his wife and daughter because their safety was imperiled by his presence. His wife being an Aryan faced no threat as long as she renounced her Jewish mate. However, their daughter was a *Mischling,* a person of mixed "race" and thus prone to deportation if found out. In fact, she was arrested a year or so later and sent to Malines. Yet she was never deported for her mother had connections and was able to get her out. She circulated among medium ranking German military who through some channel used their influence. I don't know how she happened to connect with them, but it was said that her relationship with one of the officers wasn't platonic. This she denied vehemently after the Liberation. During the years when we were hiding my uncle stopped seeing her. She later claimed to have made him stay away so as not to be accused of *Rassenschande* (disgrace brought upon one's race). On occasion, Eduard met his daughter in public places. He often returned from those encounters with many valuable goods such as *Kommissbrot*, that is, German army bread, canned meats, and fish. He offered to share with us and we tasted, but we considered this food his very private possession. Also, knowing its source made it somehow offensive. I distinctly remember feeling that way. My parents and I never spoke about it; we just knew we shared these sentiments. In any case, my uncle stayed with us for a while, then left. Sometime later he reappeared; this coming and going continued until after the Liberation.

However, at the same time we lost sight of my Cousin Max. He had moved and we didn't know his new address. I don't know when or how my parents found out that he too had been deported. [23] (See page 170.)

My uncle came to stay with us after we came back from the clothing factory to the apartment and was among us one night when I stayed up late watching a card game. As was often the case, Mme Gaby was paying us a visit for some distraction and was invited by my parents and uncle to join them in a round of rummy bridge. Seated around the kitchen table, they attempted to escape for a short while the constant haunting fear, when we heard unusual sounds coming from the street. Soon these noises became very discernible. The rumbling of motors, the clang of car and truck doors, the familiar click on the pavement of metal worn on boots conveyed the mental pictures of soldiers jumping from trucks. The Germans had returned to our street and we had no doubt as to their motive! Mme Gaby confirmed our fears; these were the same sounds she had heard some weeks before. Then she experienced again the same physical malaise that she had before - an additional confirmation. We were panic-stricken and dumbfounded; another raid after they had already been here! Our friend left quickly for her apartment to join her gentile husband as the rest of us stood horrified in our kitchen.

Only my mother had any presence of mind; she decided our course of action, and our survival was the consequence of her decisions. At a loss for any alternative, my father and uncle meekly obeyed. "Quickly, to the workshop," she urged hurriedly. Beside ourselves with fear, we hastily proceeded to the basement, leaving the apartment unlocked.

Underneath each of the two small windows of this basement room was a small closet, both of which were tiny, almost more like cupboards. My mother decided that my uncle and I should get into the cupboard hidden by the big cutting table, and that she and my father would crouch in the other. For camouflage, several sacks of fur clippings standing in a corner of the room were emptied to form mounds of fur in front of each of the small closets. I never forgot that my mother chose for me the cupboard hidden underneath the cutting table. Again my safety was her primary concern. I was very aware of her protection at the time. Although grateful, I accepted it as a given that my mother's sheltering me from danger was always her fervent intent. Her choice to put me in the safer cupboard, blocked from view by the large table, reminded me of the time she threw herself on top of me as we were machine-gunned by German aircraft during our second flight when we tried to escape the invading enemy.

I was always aware of her concern, especially so during that terrible night as I sat on my uncle's legs. With my back toward his chest, I could feel our hearts pounding as we waited. Our panic continued to increase until our teeth chattered and our bodies shook uncontrollably. The noise in the street mounted in intensity: the cries of women, furious voices, threatening shouts in German. Attempting to obliterate all consciousness to counteract my fear and shaking, I tried to shut out all sounds. But then, oh my God, I heard very clearly that they were banging at our front door, they were coming in! And, . . . oh no! I didn't want to hear, but I couldn't block out the sound of the commotion on the first floor, the heavy footsteps crossing our apartment. Nor could I shut out the thundering of more feet ascending the stairs to the upper floors. Continuously shaking, almost unconscious with fear we crouched there and waited. Soon we knew that what we had dreaded so terribly was actually happening. One of the invaders was slowly descending the basement stairs, groping his way in the dark. My mother had wisely removed all the light bulbs. We heard the familiar sound of the door handle turning and the creaking of the opening door. We held our breath. The footsteps came closer, proceeding slowly across the room. Through the cracks around the cupboard doors we saw the sheen of a flashlight moving across the floor, along the walls, and into corners. How long was the invader there ? I couldn't tell; it seemed an eternity. At last, the flashlight withdrew, the heavy footsteps slowly moved out through the doorway, and finally ascended the stairs. I allowed myself a mental sigh of relief. Could it be? Did we really elude them? Maybe they'll come back down. . ., someone else might think of verifying whether any Jews were missed. In a cold sweat, we sat as if frozen, yet continuously shaking, teeth chattering, worrying that these uncontrollable movements of our bodies might be audible and give us away. How long we remained there petrified in our cubbyholes, once more I cannot say; again it seemed an eternity. Meanwhile, I had the most desperate need to urinate. I whispered my distress to my uncle, who suggested that I relieve myself right there sitting on his legs. I was surprised and appreciative at this kindly offer, but tried to control the urge a bit longer. Finally, embarrassed and humiliated, I gave in.

Outside the sounds of slamming doors, the roaring of motors, the ugly shouting, the piteous wailing finally subsided. The trucks and cars drove off. Gradually the street assumed an eerie tranquility. Yet we didn't dare move. When dawn finally filtered through the cracks around the cupboard doors, we slowly crawled out. I observed that just like my uncle and I, my parents were shaking and their teeth were chattering. For an instant I was surprised, my childish impulse being to imagine my parents above any of my own fearful reactions. I recall my silent mental acknowledgment that the effect of terror is simply logical and natural in everyone.

No recollections remain of the immediate hours following our emergence. I recall only the bright, sunlit morning and the flabbergasted looks on our neighbors' faces, as though they had caught sight of ghosts. Mme Yvonne nearly fell through the floor. "How did you escape?" she marveled. We learned that Mme Gaby was taken away that night. "Would you believe it," wondered Mme Yvonne, "no one knew she was Jewish, not even her husband!"

Nobody ever found out why, after fooling the Germans during the first raid, Mme Gaby was arrested when they raided the second time. Later we speculated that she might have been denounced or that she might have had terrible bad luck in being questioned by a particularly scrutinizing and suspicious Nazi, who found her out. Come to think of it, just now at this writing, we may have had the good luck that the Nazi who searched the cellar was less scrupulous in his undertaking. We were able to survive because of a lucky oversight.

Mme Yvonne went on to describe the search of her apartment by three Germans. One of them, seeing her children so frightened by their presence, especially the four-year-old boy, urged the other Nazis to leave so as not to worry "the little children." My mother often recounted word for word Mme Yvonne's story about the Nazis' concern for Mme Yvonne's gentile children while persecuting and terrifying with utter disdain every Jewish child whom they captured. Later, Mme Yvonne also reported that Mme Gaby's husband had confided in her his total bewilderment and hurt. He could not comprehend why and how Mme Gaby had kept her origins a secret from him, given the many years they had shared together. He felt deceived and betrayed.

Herta arrived that morning worried and troubled. She had walked from her apartment, and arriving in the neighborhood, had noticed that every front door was marked with a cross. People on the street told her of the raid and of the way that the Germans went from house to house marking each one. We all embraced, thankful and joyful at being together and having miraculously escaped. My mother described the horrific night in detail. Just as I had expected, she also mentioned my embarrassing experience saying that I lost control and urinated out of fear. Humiliated, I protested. It had not been an accident but a dire need that I had been conscious of. Somehow, I knew that among all the horror, the others would find this a humorous interlude in the story.

And so, thinking that there might still be another raid, we returned to the clothing factory. However, this time Eduard didn't come along. He had been at the factory before, but I remember hiding there only with my parents and sister when we went back. We found the same families there and settled ourselves into another corner as best we could. At the same time we reassured everyone that we had not been followed, since being observed by some potential denouncer or some suspicious Nazi in civilian clothes was a constant danger. Therefore, as always prior to entering anywhere, we continued walking a bit farther, or around the block, assuring ourselves that no one followed.

We remained at the factory, and everything continued as it was before we left, until Herta took her ill-fated trip into town. Not only was it-ill fated, it was also a downright trap. She was lured into believing that she might find some information as to the whereabouts of her husband. Herta heard, and I don't know how, that the A. J. B. *(Association des Juifs de Belgique,* the same agency that was formed by the German occupier in June 1941 to do its dirty work) would have information regarding the whereabouts of the people who had answered the summons for compulsory work in northern France. At a specific date, time, and place, the information would be revealed to family members. Of course, Herta was eager to trace the whereabouts of her husband. I recall my mother's voicing anxiety to her at her going, and Herta replying, "it's for my husband," whereupon my mother fell silent. She left early that morning with hope and anticipation. We grew very anxious and worried after several hours had elapsed and she didn't return. As time went by, my mother became frantic. Where was Herta, she should have been back hours ago! Finally, tormented with anguish, my parents sent me to look for her. As a child I would not be noticed; furthermore unlike my parents who were hampered by language difficulties and worried about their accent, I could perhaps find some people to question.

Herta had left with us the address of her destination, as well as a phone number at the A. J. B. I have no recollection of my journey to that address. No doubt I took the streetcar as did Herta earlier. I recall finding the street and the building, nothing out of the ordinary, a house with a double door such as was often found as a front entrance. The door was unlocked. I entered a large, deserted cobblestone hallway. What should I do? I waited; not a sound. I went outside and spotted some workmen. Timidly I inquired whether they had seen anyone. They hadn't. I returned inside to look about some more, and again I waited. Oh how I prayed that I would find her, that she would appear and I would be relieved of this terrible fear and dread! Where was the pay phone that I used to call the number I had on that piece of paper? I can't remember. Yet I do remember calling at two intervals, and I can still hear the voice of the man who answered each time. I recall marveling at his cheerful "Allo," wondering how he could be so jolly. I felt terribly inadequate in providing the details of my quest. He said he knew nothing. I called the factory and spoke to my mother. I remember saying to her that this man couldn't tell me anything and her trembling voice counseling "beg him, beg him to tell you." So I called again and repeated the same questions. He reiterated, in the same animated manner, that he knew nothing and couldn't help me. I hung around in the hallway behind the double doors. As evening drew near, discouraged and feeling profoundly miserable and guilty at my inadequacy, I finally left.

I felt at fault for not having found her, for my lack of eloquence on the telephone, culpable for not having dared to inquire on the upper floors, or in the neighboring buildings. All these feelings I kept to myself. I was afraid of my parents' accusations, and I trembled in fear that they would confirm my guilt. Of course, whatever inquiries I might have made would not have changed the situation. Yet, at that time I could not have known. My inadequacy on that day plagued me until the end of my adolescence when I was finally able to figure out the situation rationally. But on that day, when I returned to the factory alone, lacking any knowledge as to what happened to my sister, I was wretched. My father met me in the courtyard. One glance at me and he knew immediately. I often wondered why certain images of the past remain indelible, almost with photographic precision. That is how I remember my father's face at that moment. His anxious eyes questioned me, and all I could do was shake my head. He started to sob, holding his head with both hands, walking to and fro as he moaned through his sobs, *"mein bestest Kind haben sie mir genommen,"* (they have taken my best child from me). Just then, my mother, who had been out, appeared. As my father went to meet her, I heard her voice trembling with apprehension, inquiring about Herta, and his negative response. The quake in her voice increasing, she said my name, and he replied that I had returned.

Seeing my parents' pain was unbearable. I had never seen my father cry; and as to my mother, she couldn't cry, and her distress was even more shattering to me. In her despair she held my father responsible for letting my sister go to that fatal meeting. *"Was hast Du mir angetan"* (what did you do to me), she lamented. My father pleaded with outstretched arms for her not to accuse him, and I cried out to her against this injustice. What followed immediately is erased from my memory. Yet I recall that I did not spend that night in the company of my parents. Another family took me under their wing for the evening and night, and I bedded down in another area of the building. I don't know at whose suggestion I did not stay with my parents, and who deemed it wiser to separate me from them as we struggled with our grief. I sat there with this family staring into space, my heart breaking. The couple's two little boys were eating apples, and the mother commented to the father about the excellence of the fruit. I didn't touch the portion of food my parents had given the woman for me, nor did I taste the apple she offered. My recollection of events at the factory ends there.

I don't know how my parents found out that my sister had indeed been arrested. She was trapped with all the others who on that day had gathered at the assigned place in the hope of learning of their loved ones' whereabouts. But they knew she was in Malines, where we sent her packages of food and clothing. From Malines came her first letter. I distinctly recall my mother's reading it aloud. We were in the kitchen of the very same apartment where we had endured the night raid. The letter came to that address (see pages 190-191).

Why did you return to that Jewish neighborhood where the Nazis raided twice already ?

We could no longer remain at the factory because the manager believed it was too dangerous, and we lacked alternatives. All the Jews in the neighborhood were gone. The lucky ones had left on their own before the raids, and the others had been caught and deported. The same people resided in the house; Mme Yvonne and her three children still lived on the third floor. Her German soldier boyfriend Fritz continued calling on her. On the second floor remained Mme Gaby's husband. I have a vague image of our kitchen, the only heated room in the apartment. My bed was moved there because I was ill with tonsillitis and my mother worried and lamented about my condition. Mme Yvonne stopped by from time to time trying to allay my mother's despondency. I was convalescing when Herta's letter arrived from Malines.

This is as good a time as any other to verify the letter in the metal box.

Not yet . . ., I am not ready to search for that letter, or any of the other letters. I know it is there, and I will get it in due time. It may be lack of courage and fear, but no matter. First I want to recount what I remember on my own, unaided.

Surprisingly, my mother's voice was firm as she read the letter that brimmed with love. My sister sang the praises of her loving family who sent her so many things. She said not to worry, not to cry. I clearly remember the words: *nicht weinen.* She also said that her wedding band and her watch were gone.[24] Then, there was a large section of her message for me. She said that it was now my job to look after our parents, since she couldn't. It was up to me to care for them, to see to their well-being and happiness. From the moment it was read to me her appeal sank deep into my consciousness. At the time I thought I could easily handle this duty, for it would be only temporary. After all, my parents were only in their late forties, they were not old. Also, I had two much older siblings with whom we would be reunited some day. I never thought that my sister might not return. Yet from that day on, I felt responsible for my parents, a feeling that lasted throughout their lives. I believe that they too started relying on me more heavily. Of course, this was mainly because of their inability to use the language; a foreign accent was a giveaway. I was their front person for all our enterprises. But in addition they expected a great deal of maturity and decision making on my part. Under the circumstances I grew up quickly. I lived up to their expectations at the ripe age of twelve.

Left to right are Régine, the author, and Estère. Brussels, May 1942. The author's two Jewish classmates, in the fifth grade, were deported with their families.

CHAPTER V

LYING

When I had recovered from my illness, my father and I went looking for other living quarters. We wanted to leave the city, and move to the outskirts, to a Flemish area where Germans would not look for Jews since normally none lived there. We took the streetcar to the end of the line, the farthest point in the district of Anderlecht. After a short walk on a road bordered by fields, we came upon a cluster of small houses. One was set apart from the others and displayed a sign A LOUER (to let) in one of the ground floor windows. A friendly man holding a young child let us in. The wife entered as we started to discuss the rooms for rent. She had obviously been listening and had observed us from another room. She had guessed our situation. The glances that she exchanged with her husband told of her disapproval, which she soon verbalized. In *Brusselik*, a dialect of Flemish mixed with French she said, *"het is geen avance"* *(il n'y a pas d'avance)*, in other words, there is no point to discuss it. They were sorry, but they could not rent to us. We realized that they would not take the chance to subject themselves to potential unpleasant and troublesome experiences. It was all very friendly, and we understood. Besides, we had expected as much.

We continued walking arbitrarily and came upon a street where on one side stood about eight small houses facing a farm-house and a long stretch of cultivated vegetable fields. In the middle of the row, one house showed another A LOUER sign. Each floor held two rooms, and the proprietor, a stout, middle-aged Flemish widow, showed us two attic rooms on the third floor. Although they were directly under the roof, the rooms were *mansardes françaises* (French attics), so called for their straight walls and windows, unlike the ordinary *mansardes*, the garrets with slanted walls and small windows that open directly onto the roof. The two windows of the larger room opened onto the wide gutter. They faced the street and offered a view of the long fields planted with vegetables. By leaning over the gutter, one could see the sidewalk below. The one window of the smaller room opened onto a view of a hill in the back of the house. The view presented a patchwork of small plots, planted by individual owners, with a variety of vegetables that spread over the hill a pleasant mixture of shapes and colors.

My father and I communicated mentally and agreed silently. We could hide in this rural neighborhood. The owner was open and frank, the house was pleasant, and the rooms light and clean. We expressed our interest and were rented the rooms on the spot, no questions asked.

The rooms were unfurnished, so we had to move some of our furniture. However, I have no clear recollection as to how we transported the few pieces from our old place to the new one. We must have brought my father's sewing machine since he used it during the years we hid there. Somehow, as I keep trying to remember the way we moved, I sense the development . . . I seem to . . . . Yes, there is the danger of imagining . . . .yet, the feeling persists, an image of my father arranging for a horse drawn cart . . . . However, I realize that I cannot trust this to be a real recollection.

But we brought Herta's large wicker trunk that she had filled with various pieces of cloth and had stored at Mme Gabin's, her neighbor on the same landing. Mme Gabin was a warm and loving, middle-aged French woman married to a Belgian. I always appreciated Mme Gabin's sensitivity in her greeting me with *bonjour ma grande* (hello my big one), instead of *ma petite* (my little one). The couple had befriended my sister and her husband. I remember that my mother and I went to claim the trunk, which stood in a corner of the Gabin's living room. When we opened it, we found on the top some of my sister's shoes and clothes. On seeing them my mother broke down and sank weeping onto a chair, holding one of my sister's shoes to her cheek. Heartbroken, I didn't know where to turn, what to do to console her. I kept repeating, "Oh Mama, Mama !" Two other sympathetic neighbors, a mother and her adult daughter who lived on the floor above, were also present at this scene. All kept repeating *"pauvre femme, pauvre femme"* (poor woman, poor woman). They offered words of encouragement and hope. We finally took the trunk when we left and carried it between us, each one holding one of its handles.

We managed to settle in our new living quarters. The countryside was peaceful. Often for hours I gazed out the smaller room's window at the patches of fields stretching out like a colorful quilt beyond the small walled-in gardens behind each house. I was surprised to find that my mother was also entranced by the view and confessed her self-indulgence in gazing out the window.

The mostly Flemish population was bilingual. On the second floor, in the two rooms below ours, lived a widow in her mid-forties with her daughter Simone, age sixteen, and her son Pierre, age eleven. Although they spoke Flemish at home, the children's schooling was all in French. The mother was very nationalistic in regard to her Flemish stock and a strict practicing Catholic. She disliked hearing her children speak French. Simone had two friends who lived on our street, farther up past a stretch of fields, in the next cluster of small houses. Henriette was a bit older than Simone, and Solange was somewhat younger. Their families were among the few in the area who spoke only French. All three girls attended the same school. Simone and Pierre's mother left early every morning in her wooden shoes to walk farther out into the countryside in search of food for her family. No one knew what she did all day and exactly where she went. Still, she always returned carrying items that were unavailable in the stores: a bit of butter, eggs, or even meat, which was the rarest of commodities. Left alone during the day, her children fended for themselves. They also befriended me.

Although Pierre was my age, I enjoyed much more the company of the sixteen-year-old Simone. I visited often, but only during the mother's absence. I sensed her irritation at my presence, which I attributed to her blaming me for her children's loafing. I really never knew exactly the reason for her irritation, but I didn't question; the three of us understood intuitively. We always watched for her appearance in the evening at the top of the street, when she came back from her day in the country. I then left my new friends and returned to our rooms above theirs.

This was the time when my identity had to be totally reinvented. There was no family council to decide what to say. Since I had the most contact with people, I was the spokesperson. I felt I had to explain to the landlady the reason for my parents' accent and their lack of fluency in French, so I simply said that we had come from Austria to live in Belgium. Otherwise, it was left up to me to camouflage our past. But I never premeditated, I invented spontaneously as I went from one lie to the next, remembering what I had said, then building on more lies. Fortunately, I could rely on my good memory. I knew our safety depended on it. Unknowingly, I found that the best way to remember was to build for myself the identity I longed for, yet one that was logical and believable to strangers. Jewish children couldn't go to school, but I said I was a pupil at the *Ecole Moyenne* (Middle School), the school in our district that I most wanted to attend. This chosen identity was my Ariane's thread. In addition, I replaced my totally foreign sounding first name with "Irène." My parents practiced calling me by this new name in order to get used to it, so as not to give me away in front of our new circle of neighbors.

I was anxious and feared being perceived as a liar. Lying made me unhappy and uncomfortable, and I often despised myself. What to say next to cover the lie became a challenge, until I was totally entangled in a fictitious existence, so much so that since I wished to be that person so badly, I came to feel that I was in some way that other me who kept gaining strength over my true identity. But all along there persisted inside the nagging guilt, the feeling of imprisonment in deception.

Weren't the people in the house suspicious when they did not hear or see you leave for school in the morning and return in the afternoon? Also, the Ecole Moyenne that you said you attended was not far from Simone's, Henriette's, and Solange's school. Didn't they wonder why they never met you on the street or in the streetcar?

Luckily, "my school" started and ended at a slightly different time than theirs. I worried all the same, but I knew that I had no other alternative. I could only pretend to have left in the morning, but I could not actually leave. There was nowhere for me to spend the day safely. I decided I couldn't do anything in case they wondered why they never met, heard, or saw me leave, or return from school. My only option was to remain hidden in our rooms during those hours. I never ventured out, not even as far as the hallway or our landing, until after the proper hour of my fictitious return.

And no one ever questioned you?

I was preoccupied with the thought and sometimes imagined that someone would. On the other hand, I felt a certain discretion on the part of others, or was it just indifference? Again, I had to accept the situation even though I worried. All I could do was keep out of sight during the school day. I read for hours anything and everything I could find in the private lending library run in a used bookstore nearby. I pored over not only all the classic French children's books but also many of the nineteenth-century French novels, as well as some of the contemporary tabloid best-sellers that I picked from a stack according to the picture on the cover, or a catchy title. The store proprietor's face sometimes expressed misgivings at allowing a child of my age to borrow such books. I understood his hesitation and alleviated his uncertainties by saying that the novels were for my mother and older sister. I don't think I convinced him - still, he didn't stop me. Of course, I didn't understand a large part of what I read, but through those books, the good ones and the bad ones, I became an avid reader, and at the same time obtained a large part of my education regarding relationships between the sexes. That is how I was "enlightened" about human sexuality and mores, in a way as twisted as our hidden existence.

Around four o'clock in the afternoon I listened for Simone's and Pierre's return. I would conveniently be getting water from our hall faucet because Simone always called for me to come down when she heard me. At times she called from their open terrace below our smaller room. I liked being with her. In her mother's absence we listened to the radio and learned the latest tunes. She gossiped about boys, neighbors, friends, and teachers.

You went out frequently. Could that have been why people were not suspicious, because you seemed to be living "normally"?

We came and went, usually in search of food. We had mostly vegetables bought from the farmer across the way. We went for walks, either in the fields or in the cemetery through which we could reach a commercial area. Yet that constant fear was always present, that feeling of intense vulnerability, the sense of panic at the sight of a suspicious-looking black automobile. The fear of being followed and denounced by someone who suspected that we were Jews was continually with us. Sometimes, out of boredom, I joined Simone and Pierre at Sunday mass; it gave me something to examine. At times Simone took me along to the girls' division of the JOC *Jeunesse Ouvrière Chrétienne* (Working-class Christian Youth). She despised those gatherings but attended at her mother's urging. Simone often said to her that she had been at the JOC when we both had gone to the local movie instead. The theater was within walking distance, and on occasion my parents and I went together. Of course, Jews were barred from all theaters. Each box office displayed prominently a sign reading *Entrée interdite aux Juifs* (Entry forbidden to Jews). The German occupier forced these signs upon the population. They were displayed by law but ignored by patrons as well as managers and personnel. The Germans were our common enemy. The gentile Belgians did not fear them as we did, since they were not persecuted as long as they showed no overt opposition. But the Belgians disliked them intensely.

I may have made up stories about my own teachers and classmates, but I don't recall any specific ones. I don't think I said very much, I just worried about it. Luckily Simone was self-absorbed and contented to speak about herself. I thought then that she didn't care and that she remained fooled. In retrospect I am not so sure, given the fact that she was fairly astute. She must have wondered why I had so little to say about my own school days.

Finding some of these people and asking them remains a possibility, but it would entail intense detective work. Unfortunately, I remember only their first names and don't know what became of them. It is surprising that I recall names of people whom I met much earlier, whereas the names of others whom I had met much later, when I was older, have disappeared from my memory. I have tried to find an explanation, and upon reflection I concluded that the names I recall are of people involved with at least one member of my family as well as myself. I don't remember names when my relationships excluded my family. Moreover, what is true of forgetting names is true of events as well. Many episodes of my earlier childhood stand out clearly. Others that happened later have faded to the point of leaving at best only an impression of the event, or they have vanished altogether. It may be true that I have unintentionally erased the most painful time of my childhood. I might have pushed it back as far as possible into the furthest sphere of my consciousness. I refused to think of it, let alone talk about it. This could be partly the reason why I cannot recall the name of the convent and the school I finally attended during that time. The logical reason for my amnesia is the mental and emotional anguish that I endured at that school. I used much psychic energy to blot out those memories. Even the name of the girl who initiated my presence there escaped me for a long time. It suddenly resurfaced while I spoke of my experiences to a group of university students. Yes, during that presentation it occurred to me that her name was Louise, yet I am not absolutely certain. However, I will refer to her by that name; still, I cannot recall her last name.

Louise was a blond and blue-eyed Jewish girl whom I knew from public school where she and I were pupils before Jewish children were barred from attending. We had lost sight of each other, and then we met again by chance in the street. I was with my mother in search of shops that might carry some provisions that day. Usually all shelves were bare, but occasionally, no one knew exactly when, some stores received a shipment of some kind of food. We stopped to chat, happy to see the familiar face of someone who had also so far eluded the Nazis. She lived close by to where we met. She said that her mother had placed her and her younger brother separately in hiding with gentile couples. Her father had been caught by the Nazis and deported, but her mother was hiding somewhere else. Louise didn't like the people with whom she stayed; therefore she was glad to spend much of her time at a convent school. The nuns had accepted her clandestinely. Thus I learned that this convent was in the countryside fairly close to were we lived. My friend needed to come by streetcar, but it would be within walking distance for me. Louise urged me to join her: "I am the only Jew there, come to my class. Go and see the mother superior . . . ," she said.

The sisters' convent stood among a cluster of tan and brick buildings comprising a church, a small chapel, a girls' boarding school and dormitories, and a day school. The residents of the boarding school, who came from well-to-do families, enjoyed some recreational facilities, among others a fenced-in roller-skating rink. The girls' day school was run separately from the boarding school. It serviced the children from the area's farming and working-class communities. The boarding school recreational facilities were unavailable to the students of the day school, who frequently stood outside the high chain-link fence in the hollow trench that surrounded the rink and watched the uniformed girls skate. The day school had a nice cemented school yard for recess. Its building, hallways, and classes were bright and clean.

I only faintly recall my interview with the mother superior; I know it was brief. Yet I distinctly remember a vagueness about her. I sensed a lack of connection, an absence of intensity. Moreover, I found the severe black habit estranging and intimidating. The religious statues, paintings, and decorations in her office and in the building made me ill at ease. Still, she was friendly and smiled a great deal. I met the lay teacher, a pleasant woman probably in her early thirties, though she may have been younger. Children often misjudge the age of adults. I was relieved to see her ordinary clothing. Her complexion reminded me of a ripe apple. She wore her thick light brown hair in a *"rouleau,"* that is, rolled up around her head. I found her large blue eyes reassuring. I liked her - I thought that her kindness and concern were truly genuine. She assured me that only she and the mother superior would know of my origins. In her classroom where I first sat to observe, my clandestine Jewish friend greeted me enthusiastically. The curriculum was conducted entirely in Flemish. French was taught twice a week, the reverse from my previous school where classes were entirely in French, and Flemish was studied two times a week.

I consulted my parent, who encouraged me to go. "At least you'll learn something," they said. Also, I considered the relief of not having to hide all day. I would be seen and heard leaving and returning home. Moreover, Simone's and Pierre's schools still had a different schedule, so I didn't have to worry about their wondering why they never met me coming or going. I told no one of my "new school," anticipating bewilderment at my attending there.

At first I refrained from participating in class. The teacher gave me time to familiarize myself with my new surroundings. Although I had enjoyed Flemish earlier in school, a total immersion in the language required extra attention. This was so for Louise as well, and the other pupils seemed to accept the explanation. However, I harbored an uneasy feeling. I knew that the children were not stupid, and some of them seemed rather shrewd. I feared their curiosity. How could they fail to wonder why these two middle-class French-speaking girls suddenly came to this isolated, rural Flemish school? They might speak of us at home or in the presence of some friends of their families, perhaps sympathizers of the Germans who might inquire at the school, find out that we are Jewish, and denounce us. Thus I always remained guarded and skeptical, on constant alert. In addition, I grew increasingly more uncomfortable with the religious trappings. Contrary to my friend Louise who willingly participated in all the rituals, I was alienated and disturbed by having to say the many prayers in class, having to cross myself, to listen to catechism lessons twice daily, and frequently attending church services. My confidence in my teacher dropped sharply following a brief discussion in the school yard during recess. I never forgot her words to me that day. She said she hoped that I would eventually realize that her religion was the true religion. I knew that she meant well, and I never doubted her personal sincerity. Still, by then I mistrusted her and suspected ulterior motives on her part.

My connection with the school remained exclusively with the classroom teacher whom I liked, after all. I seldom had any contact with the Mother Superior, whom I saw occasionally in passing in the school yard, the halls, during assembly, or when my class was in church. She always smiled, but I sensed her distance. Perhaps she knew of my skepticism. The thought occurred to me sometimes that I was the subject of discussion between her and my teacher. I think the Mother Superior knew of my reluctance. No doubt the teacher noticed that my mind turned off completely during catechism class. All the same, her words floated in the room, seeming to hover over me. I tried to dismiss them as best I could by directing my thoughts elsewhere. Yet some of her comments penetrated the shield I had erected. If they never convinced me, I never forgot them either. A particular discussion about salvation stubbornly persisted, such as when she elaborated on the concept of recognition of Christ as God. She said that all Christians must constantly reiterate this belief. In case of accidental death, in case last rites could not be administered, it was sufficient that this thought just flash through one's mind in order to be saved. No other subject studied there left an imprint on my memory except religion. Nothing stands out with regard to any academic subject. The reason may be that no effort was ever required, for I don't recall any intellectual challenges or gratifying achievements. The subjects I remember during the time spent there are the ones that made me uncomfortable.

Sometimes I observed with my classmates the girls of the boarding school in the skating rink. They commented about those students' fortunate material situation compared with their own. Nevertheless, they never questioned the validity of their place in their own social class. The difference between them and the girls of the boarding school was a simple fact; they belonged to another category in society. The justice of the matter was never questioned. As far as I was concerned, I never harbored any resentment regarding the privileged facilities accorded to the students of the boarding school. I had no wish to enter the world of those children; I desired no part of it, no more than the world of the day school children. The only aspect of their lives that I envied was their freedom from Nazi persecution, their peace of mind. Otherwise I never wished to be one of them, or among them. All my striving consisted in maintaining the ability of my parents and myself not to be caught or denounced. Just to hold on long enough in hiding until the defeat of the enemy.

Life at school became increasingly more difficult for me as Easter drew near, because of the many rituals in preparation for the holiday. The intensity and length of the lessons in religion increased noticeably as did attendance at church services. I remember that during one such service, after the teacher had led the class to assigned rows of seats, I could not bring myself to participate in two required rituals. The first was when she signaled to the students in each row to file out one by one and await their turn in line to walk to the front of the nave and prostrate at the foot of the crucifix. I recall the shock at the practice of this religious rite. It seemed to me so exaggerated, so fanatical. I could not do it. I remained standing in my row as all my classmates filed out past me.

Unfortunately, the teacher had never prepared me. Had she warned me as to what to expect, I could have controlled my reaction. I had never thought of this possibility until this writing. Yes, the teacher lacked sensitivity, perhaps even intelligence, but above all she lacked experience. Obviously, she had never been confronted with such a situation. Most probably she expected the same behavior from me as from Louise, who joined in all the rites without any apparent difficulty. Louise showed no reluctance, and I often thought she secretly enjoyed participating. In any case, Louise never voiced any objections to me. She knew of mine, but we never discussed the matter. Our eyes met as she returned to her seat after prostrating herself like the others. Our glances signaled that we simply understood that I minded and that she didn't.

The teacher may have spoken of the ritual in class and therefore thought that I was prepared. But I heard nothing, probably because I paid no attention and blocked it all out as much as possible. However, even if she had spoken about it in class, it would have been wise on her part to speak to me separately. She may have hesitated because she remembered the time when she said to me that I would come to see that her religion is the true one. She probably realized then that her comments were clumsy, and knew that they had put me off. Consequently, she may have been at a loss as to what explanation to give me.

Yet she was not so obtuse. She saw that often when I had to make the sign of the cross, I would turn away and trying not to be seen, wipe it off. She took me aside and cautioned me that the other students might notice when I did that. For whatever reason, and there may have been several, she never imparted any instructions to me personally before I was faced with a new experience of religious rites. It was unfortunate, because I was left to confront rituals I found objectionable and frightening. The second astonishing event of which I had no previous warning was the students' expected communion during that same religious service. I only guessed at what was happening, why everyone again lined up, slowly walked forward with hands folded. I guessed that it was to receive the Eucharist. I assumed this to be the rite I read about in those nineteenth-century French novels that I brought home from the private lending library. My heart sank in alarm. Again, I did not move from my row as everyone else walked past me.

But on Good Friday you knelt with everyone else. Why wasn't it objectionable to you then?

Again, I was very uncomfortable. Yet the fact that the ritual didn't take place in church made it less objectionable. Also, I have a notion that I knew of the plan beforehand. It was discussed in class, and I paid attention then. Several minutes before Christ was supposed to have died on the cross, we descended the stairs in silence, two by two, to stand in the school yard. The children remained according to the classroom's seating order. The teacher focused on her wristwatch. At a specific moment she signaled, and everybody fell to their knees. Standing among my classmates, I had no alternative but to kneel as well. This time in some way, I was able inwardly to distance myself from my actions. I recall consciously dismissing the symbolism of the gesture. I also attended the class festivities on Easter Sunday morning in the school's large parlor. I recall a bright sunlit room, and except for the religious statuary and paintings of which I was continually aware, I found the room comfortable and fitting for the occasion. The Mother Superior and our teacher hosted the event. Two other sisters attended also. Two male church dignitaries honored the class with their presence, including a priest in traditional black garb whom I saw occasionally on the school grounds, and someone of higher rank in more colorful attire, the subject of noticeable excitement among the sisters and students. I glanced at him from time to time. He was a heavy-set, middle-aged man. He had a ruddy complexion, and the circle of graying hair surrounding his bald head augmented the roundness of his face and added to the total rotund appearance of his person. He smiled a great deal, apparently very pleased with the children's performance. There was choral singing and one of the girls recited a poem celebrating the resurrection of Christ. I can still hear the Flemish words of the first line:

Oh Heer, ik ben blij dat Gij gerenzen zij.

(Oh Lord, I am happy that you have risen.)

Who was this dignitary? His title and name were surely mentioned. But the matter was of no interest to me, and I remained mentally distant throughout. My observations which were ordinarily keen, remained subconsciously vague. The occasion and who was present left me indifferent. I had no desire to speak to anyone and remained inconspicuous.

Did any of the visitors know your secret?

Who knew of my origins was a matter of constant concern to me; therefore, I was hypersensitive to any mental vibrations around me. I observed the visitors from the corner of my eye, especially the dignitary. I thought that he most likely knew nothing about me, and that if he did know anything, it was imperceptible. However, I had only my intuition to go by. All the adults present were involved with the celebration, and no more attention was paid to me than to the others, except for the children who performed solos. I withdrew into the background physically as well as mentally and left at the earliest opportunity.

It was inevitable that your attitude would be noticed and questioned by your classmates.

I put to use all my acting talents so as not to show my feelings. Generally, I just assumed an air of indifference. Still, the two aforementioned incidents in church, when I abstained from participating in the rituals, resulted in igniting the curiosity of two girls in particular. The perseverance of one of them was especially troubling. The fact that I had not taken communion along with everyone else sparked her interest, and ever so often she quizzed me with seeming casualness. Did I celebrate my first communion? When I answered in the affirmative, she inquired where it took place. Thinking fast and seeming unperturbed, I named Ste Gudule, a church I had passed by once while on a walk with my sister and her friend. They had discussed its architecture. It was located in one of Brussels's fashionable areas in the center of town. I guessed at the girl's ignorance of that part of the city. My quick response left her perplexed for a while. I had the distinct feeling that she did not believe me. Later she wanted to know where I was baptized. Again I cited the same church. Thus she recurrently queried me, and I kept inventing the answers. Still, she was not satisfied and continued what seemed to develop into an investigation. Some of the other girls' attitudes indicated that she gossiped about me. She spread the rumor that I lied. I sensed in her behavior that she would press me until she obtained satisfaction in her quest, whatever and whenever that might be. The situation became increasingly more painful for me. It was terribly stressful, and I was very unhappy. Sometimes I sought relief by skipping school. When I returned and the teacher inquired as to my absence she told me how worried she was every time I missed class. When she did not see me, she feared that I had been caught by the Germans. She knew of my difficulty with my classmates and my deep, all encompassing sadness. She then made two more remarks I thought peculiar. She said I should consider that some of my present unhappiness might work to relieve the suffering of my deported sister, my aunt, and my cousins. She advised me to regard some of my endured sadness as a consolation, for it might relieve the trouble of my loved ones. I never doubted the sincerity of her advice and her empathy. I thought that her counsel was appealing, a way of circumventing difficult circumstances. Yet I knew it was unrealistic, a kind of wishful thinking that I could not believe. On another occasion, as I kept building my fictional Christian persona and thus added lie upon lie to my tale, another of her remarks left me totally perplexed and very hurt. Our conversations usually took place in the school yard - they were brief interchanges. During one such dialogue, she told me that I must understand that her religion forbade her to lie. Her comment immediately stirred up a multitude of feelings and thoughts. Its primary effect was to increase my already profound sense of culpability and self-hatred, and to deepen my depression. In addition, they increased my suspicion and my defensiveness. How could she say that? Did she mean that my religion, contrary to hers, condoned lying? Or was she implying that her religion emphasized truth more than mine? The words she had spoken when I first came echoed in my mind: "You will see that my religion is the true religion." Perhaps she assumed that lying did not matter to me, when in fact it disturbed me deeply. I despised having to invent additional accounts to give sequence to the stories already told. I recall the ever-present and growing empty inner feeling that each falsification left within me. At times I longed for some of my inventions to be true, for then I would be like everyone else, would not have to hide, would not have to lie. Yet this yearning only augmented my inner emptiness. Now everything about me was false. I disliked who I was but could not be otherwise.

Of course, you were incapable of such introspection. All you knew was that you were unhappy.

I knew exactly why I was wretched and was conscious of all my yearnings for normalcy. Perhaps if I had been asked why I was unhappy there, I might have given as reasons my classmates' suspicions, their queries, and their gossip about me. This was not only depressing, but dangerous as well. I always worried about who might hear. I believed my teacher was aware of my feelings.

Was she obtuse and clumsy, or was she irritated with you and somewhat vindictive? Her words were certainly cruel under the circumstances.

I never thought of her in that way then. Her tone was kind, and I never questioned her concern for me. Although surprised by her ingenuousness, I really doubted that she would apply her religious teachings unconditionally. Yes, I thought that her remark lacked honesty. But, in addition, I remember concluding that she did not comprehend my mental and emotional predicament, but I excused her. After all, I thought, she never had needed to flee or hide, so she couldn't know what it meant to be persecuted. She had never experienced the terror of such an existence. But all along I had mixed feelings and was perturbed because this development was dangerous and could not be disregarded. I kept wondering whether her faith would really compel her not to lie if ever confronted by the Germans regarding Louise and

I. Would her religion actually oblige her to tell them who we were?

Did you question her on the matter?

At the moment I didn't think the remark worthwhile discussing. More importantly, I wanted to be respectful and feared that what I said might embarrass her. Although worried, I let it pass but made an additional mental note to be constantly vigilant.

Did you speak to Louise? After all this concerned her too.

I knew that unlike me, Louise was not ill at ease. I didn't involve her in my misgivings. My parents were aware of my difficulties. I recall my mother's repeating to my father my teacher's notion that my own distress might possibly serve, by some divine design, to lessen the suffering of my deported sister or other members of my family. My parents' faces expressed amazement at this conception. They found the idea lacking in common sense. But they couldn't guide me in my struggle. They opted to leave all initiative to me, to support my decisions, and to let me follow my intuition. Although I don't remember any specific discussion, I knew their sentiments regardless. Intuitively I understood their sense of disorientation. Therefore, it was often necessary for me to assume, albeit with great insecurity, choices for all of us as well as for myself.

My parents never interfered with my outings with Simone and her friends Solange and Henriette. On Sunday we sometimes took the streetcar to go walking in the center of Brussels, or to see a movie there. When I think of the anxiety they must have endured until my return, I wonder how they could have let me go. Most likely they saw that I needed distractions and trusted that I would be camouflaged by the company of these older, obviously gentile Belgian girls. I felt their concern for my isolation, yet I often wondered at their confidence in my instincts. How often, when I was with my friends, did my heart stop at the sight of foreboding automobiles or uniformed SS in the streets, or when spotting a swastika in the lapel of what was clearly a German in civilian clothes, probably from the Gestapo? I did not reveal to my parents these encounters and my fears. As adults, how much more anxiety they must have endured, how much greater must have been the fear and loss that disoriented them. Optimism and confidence make up a child's outlook so that even under dire circumstances, a child's mentality tends toward hope. Perhaps that was why I acted so often to fill a void and took leadership at so young an age.

They followed my directions on many occasions. One such occurrence was when we encountered the most obnoxious of my classmates, the one most suspicious and curious about me. We were walking on a Sunday through the fields and the rural neighborhood when I heard someone call, Irène, Irène. . .! As I turned, I saw her at some distance running toward us. She had recognized me by my clothes since I had so few, they always seemed the same. I knew that she wanted to inspect my parents, and I had to prevent her from doing so. Of course, their accent and lack of fluency in the language would engender more questions and only force me to come up with more lies. "Quickly," I said to them, "you cannot let her spy on you, you must disappear from sight." Luckily they were able to turn a corner and vanish before she reached me.

How disappointed she was when she found me waiting for her by myself. Indeed, her face fell. She definitely had expected to discover something interesting. She inquired about my parents' whereabouts. I explained that they needed to go home but that I had remained to wait for her, since I had heard her call my name and had seen her running towards me, thinking she may have something to tell me. Of course she had nothing to say. We chatted briefly and then separated. I felt she suspected that my parents sought to avoid her. The encounter may have caused her to embellish the gossip about me. The tattling increased progressively and ultimately brought the interference of the Mother Superior. I never knew whether she had heard the gossip herself or whether the teacher had kept her apprised of my difficulties all along. In retrospect, I believe the latter. At the time I may have speculated about it. However, since the subject was so unpleasant, I simply blocked it out.

Standing near the teacher's desk on a platform facing the children, the Mother Superior gave a speech. No doubt she assumed that her intervention would stop the speculation. From where I sat, her slight, black-garbed silhouette stood profiled against one of the sunlit windows. One sentence from the sum of her speech struck me like lightning. She said, "Saint Mary is the mother of all children, believers as well as nonbelievers." I was petrified. No doubt, everyone understood what she implied, and who this "nonbeliever" was. I thought, "My God, she gave me away. How could she be so ignorant? The children will tell their parents, and they in turn may tell others, perhaps collaborators of the Nazis. For if I am a nonbeliever, what am I doing in a Catholic school? I can no longer stay here." I thought that her intentions were good, but that she had not weighed the possible consequences. I was convinced that the implications of her speech were foolish and dangerous.

How did the children react?

I don't know, for I looked at no one. I thought only of disappearing as soon as possible. This episode probably took place at the end of the school day, since I recall no subjects studied afterwards. Yet it may very well be that this single event erased all other memory of what followed on that day. It was to be the last of my tribulations there, yet the psychological repercussions were numerous, damaging, and long-lasting. From that day on I didn't return to the school until after liberation, to pay a courtesy call.

Did you wonder how Louise was able to stay?

Louise was not happy living with the middle-aged gentile couple with whom her mother had hidden her. She was reasonably content at school, considering the alternative of remaining with these people all day. We never sought each other out, but later met twice by chance in the street. Our first encounter occurred while we were still under the Nazi occupation. She said that in school the gossip about me had gone on for some time and that a few of my former classmates had often confronted her and had called me a big liar. We made light of those girls and laughed. After all, we knew we were both forced to lie. Yet, for me the old deep hurt came back. Louise meant only to inform me and was not aware of my distress. When we parted, I asked her to convey my regards to the teacher.

We met the second time after liberation. It was then that she fully apprised me of the many changes she had undergone since I had left the school. Louise had been baptized under the sisters' guidance without her mother's knowledge. She became a devoted Catholic and executed all the required rituals and sacraments. After Brussels was liberated by the Allied armies she was reunited with her mother and brother, and enrolled in a secular school. But she insisted on continuing to go to church, especially to Sunday mass. Her mother would not hear of it, forbade it. Nevertheless, Louise managed to sneak out and went anyway. The relationship between mother and daughter grew very tense. However, with the mother's perseverance, the girl relented little by little. She made other friends and under their influence joined a Zionist youth organization which happened to be opposed to all religious ideology. When Louise returned to visit the convent school, she had by then become an atheist. To the amazement of her former teacher and some sisters, she proceeded to enlighten them with the theory of evolution. As they objected and argued, she stubbornly kept explaining the formation of cells. This, then, was Louise at our second encounter, happy and free, a dedicated Zionist and an atheist.

When I visited the convent school, my converted friend was the subject of our former teacher's lament and regret. Yes, she said, they shouldn't have given in to her plea to be baptized, they shouldn't have done it. She could not have understood, she was too young. And now, tragically, she is a nonbeliever constantly postulating about one silly cell or another. At least you, she added, still believe in God. I answered in the affirmative. Louise had already told me of her visit and of her reception there. Although I understood the woman's good will, I had little empathy with her remorse.

When I decided to leave after the Mother Superior's talk, I faced a return to the general boredom, among many other stresses. Once more I had to remain hidden in our rooms and to pretend to be in school. Naturally, the boredom and the isolation were demoralizing, but at least I was spared the constant pressures and mental discomfort. I returned to the lending library and resumed reading everything I could find.

CHAPTER VI

HIDING

For several days a week shortly after the noon hour, I left
our rooms, pretending, according to custom, to return to
school after the midday meal. My mother and I walked from
our rural district through the large cemetery leading to the
dwelling of some acquaintances. Their old storefront house
concealed the remnants of an extended Jewish family, all of
whom had also fled from Austria to Belgium. It housed a
couple in their mid thirties, their seven-year-old son, the
woman's father, and the husband's two single sisters in their
early thirties. Franzi, the younger sister, was hunchbacked;
Minna, the older one, was very short and squat. Both of
them had been stunted in their growth by some birth defect.
They were alert and bright, warm and good hearted women.
Selma, another sister in her early forties, whose husband had
been deported, also lived with them. But the boy's grandmother and his mother's two little sisters, Trudi, about thirteen, and Grete about eleven (renamed in school *Gertrude*
and *Marguerite*) were absent. The two girls had been my playmates and schoolmates. The whole Schönfeld family was
summoned when the persecution of Jews started. Because
the father had a lung ailment, he was at the time able to be
exempt. However, fearing retribution, the mother took the
two children, and two other daughters in their early twenties, and reported with all of them to Malines. Of course,
those who remained wanted to believe, like the rest of us

with deported loved ones, that they would see them again.[25] The in-law members of the Schönfelds, whose last name was Sonnenfeld, had left the old neighborhood and had found this area to live in hiding. All the adults had worked in the manufacturing of leather goods, and at the time still had a remaining source supplying them with piecework at home. This enabled them at least to survive. They cheerfully welcomed visitors, who in turn took great care to be certain not to have been followed or observed before entering their dwelling. From time to time they also harbored overnight acquaintances who, worried that their concealed identity had been discovered or that they had been denounced to the Germans, came asking for shelter. They stayed until they found other lodgings, or in case of false alarm, left when they thought that it was safe to return to the old ones.

The harboring of acquaintances who feared disclosure of their secret locality to the Germans was a common occurrence among Jews in hiding. In particular, I recall the arrival at our own dwelling one summer evening of the Littmans, a German Jewish refugee couple who had placed their young daughter with a gentile couple. They pleaded to be allowed to spend the night "no more than on a chair," in the woman's words. Naturally my parents consented and bedded them down on the floor as best they could. My uncle Eduard stayed with us off and on for various lengths of time. Of course, he knew that our place was always an alternative for him. The Sonnenfelds had several contacts with people in hiding. Their open house policy was customary. At the start of the persecutions in the summer of 1942, their extended family's home had sheltered young children whose parents could not look after them. They also lodged Otto, a sweet boy of about sixteen whose last name I cannot remember. Somehow he was alone in Belgium, his divorced parents having escaped separately from Austria to other countries. I remember his coming to say goodbye the day before he answered the Nazis' summons.

In the latter part of 1943 and in 1944, we often met at the Sonnenfelds' secret hideout with two or three of the same regular visitors looking for distraction and sociability. They arrived while their hosts were still cutting and stitching the imitation leather goods on order. When work was done, they set up the table for the ever ongoing rummy bridge card game. But only the honor of winning was at stake in this pastime. Popular songs and old Viennese melodies often accompanied the card playing. All these distractions acted as a further mental escape from the ever present consciousness of persecution. I only watched the playing, but I always joined in the singing.

It was there that I experienced my first teaching assignment. The little boy's parents invited me to instruct their seven - or by then eight-year-old son. He had had no schooling, and neither of his parents nor other family members were inclined by temperament or patience to teach. I didn't think myself worthy of the job. I was thirteen by then, and having been deprived for so long of instruction myself, I felt ignorant and had very low self-esteem. I thought I could never catch up and would forever be uneducated. Again I spoke to no one about my concern; it was my own problem, and nothing could be done. At the time I knew it was not important to my parents. The main concern was to survive - everything else had low priority. Yet the Sonnenfelds considered me worthy and thought highly of me. Flattered at their confidence, I accepted. Nevertheless, again I felt deceitful because I gave an appearance of maturity and capability, and yet I felt so deeply insecure.

The lesson lasted from two to four o'clock, with a break for our *goûter,* as my pupil and I who conversed solely in French called the light meal. We studied in one of the bare rooms on the upper floors. There, either the boy's mother or his father brought us our *Jause*, the German word used by all the adults, the only language they spoke fluently. The meal consisted of a slice of dark bread dabbed with either margarine or some thin preserve, and a cup of imitation coffee made of chicory and ground, roasted dried peas. In this way many people replaced the usual required ingredients for the beverage. When the drink was sweetened, it tasted wonderful to us, two hungry children. The meal was payment for my instruction. I relished my salary and anticipated it eagerly every time.

My pupil's name was Heinz, but everyone called him by the diminutive Heinzi. For me he was Henri, the French translation of his German name. He liked me very much despite my scolding and shouting in frustration when he didn't understand the exercise. I recall his smiling face; he probably never took my reprimand seriously. Perhaps his positive nature overcame my reproving and never discouraged him. At first I worried about being heard on the floor below, as indeed I was. Yet to my surprise all the adults greatly approved of my "energetic" way of instruction. To them it proved my "seriousness" that, in their opinion, would bring good results. Of course, I could show my pupil only the fundamentals of arithmetic, writing, and reading. I had no textbooks and had to make up the material as we went along. When the lesson was over, we played or engaged in long conversations. He saw in me a big friend, not only just his teacher.

Sadly, the tale about little Henri has a tragic conclusion. Following Liberation, after we all emerged from hiding, my former pupil was hit by a motorcyclist and died. During our pupil-teacher relationship I had no real affinity for young children, but I had great affection for him. Had I been older and more knowledgeable I would have noticed special attributes about him, particularly his unusual sunny disposition. At the time I thought that he was just a normal little boy, nondescript like so many seven-year-olds. I remember thinking only that his complexion was so very fair, given his brown eyes and hair.

How could the Jews in hiding purchase food? Everyone needed ration cards issued by the Belgian authorities.

People never changed the address that they had declared on the day they registered for ration cards when the system was implemented for the total population at the start of the occupation. Without ration stamps it was impossible to survive. Therefore, every month people took on the potentially dangerous task of collecting the ration stamps allotted to every ration card. On November 24, 1943, at the City Hall of one of the district of greater Brussels named St.-Gilles, where ration stamps were being distributed, Jews were tracked down by Nazi police. This method had already been tried by the Nazis in the city of Antwerp, where it scandalized the office personnel, who objected to being used as bait.[26] It was in part a result of the refusal of the Belgian authorities to participate in the enemies' oppression of Jews that people lucky enough to elude their persecution managed to survive. The authorities distributed the stamps to whoever presented a ration card.

The Sonnenfelds also had other means. They had a gentile Belgian acquaintance who dealt in the black market of various food commodities that were scarce or absent from grocery store shelves. The family members pooled their resources from their piecework to purchase from their friend the foods that he sold to them at reduced prices.

We had to manage solely with the ration cards, although the rations were meager, and the food which was almost always of miserable quality, was often unavailable. We were all badly undernourished, but the ration stamps made survival possible. My father went to collect them in connection with our former domicile which of course we never officially reported changed.

Thanks to my father's versatility and talent to adapt to different types of work, my parents could pay rent for our attic rooms and could purchase the meager rations of food available with ration stamps. He sought out former connections in the fur and garment industries. Through them and intermediary sources he found work. At first he undertook the treacherous daily commute to workshops located in seeming "safe" areas of town. In order not to attract attention, he would leave early in the morning when it was still dark, and would return after dark in the evening. Later he did piece-work at home on his sewing machine with my mother helping in various ways. He picked up bundles of precut men's coats and jackets to be assembled. This was often a frustrating task because of the low-grade material, mostly imitation of one kind or another. He would deliver the finished work and return with a new lot. Of course we had no choice but to deal with the ever-present fear and danger of evil encounters. However, our coming and going gave us the semblance of leading a normal life. As mentioned before, perhaps this seeming normalcy was enough to avoid arousing our neighbors' suspicion and to mask our situation.

One cold winter day during one of my father's journeys, my mother and I experienced another of our many frightful plights. Suddenly we heard the sound of automobiles. Bending over the gutter that ran below our two windows overlooking the street, we saw two black sedans that had come to a stop a few houses away. At once we rushed down the stairs, throwing on our coats as we left the house. Forcing ourselves to appear casual, we briskly walked in a matter-of-fact manner in the opposite direction. As I followed my mother, I noticed how the heels of her sling-back sandals scattered snow into the only shoes she possessed. But then we heard motors behind our backs, and two black cars sped by. In the back seat of the last car we saw three men. In the middle sat the hairdresser who worked on the corner - a man in his late twenties or early thirties who lived with his parents. He ran his shop in their private house. I had been there once when he cut my mother's hair. I had felt then an unusual atmosphere in that house, something strange about the parents and the son. The house was dark, the shades were drawn, and the people, although friendly, were subdued, as if somehow fearful. As the cars rushed by, I noticed that our hairdresser neighbor sat bareheaded between two, presumably Gestapo men, who wore conventional men's felt hats. The fearful atmosphere in the house made sense to me now. The man was probably in the Belgian underground and the Gestapo had come to arrest him. Luckily, the Nazis knew nothing about us. After Liberation, our neighbor returned, having survived the concentration camp. We then learned that our intuition had been correct. Indeed, the man was a Resistance fighter.

We received some additional messages from Herta, two of which I remember clearly. Both of them were letters that she threw out of the train en route to Auschwitz, although at the time she didn't know her destination. I believe my father retrieved them at our former address. (Please see the Epilogue, pages 190-191.) One of the letters was written in pencil on the inside of the jacket that had contained her wedding picture, which she had with her when she was caught. On the outside of the jacket she addressed the finder in French, begging that person to forward her missive. It was sent to us with a note, *Ils sont partis vers l'est* (they have gone toward the east), at the bottom of the outside of the picture jacket. The second letter was addressed to the finder with whom she pleaded in German to forward her message to her family. She appealed to that person's compassion for distressed parents who pine for a sign of life from their child. Both times decent souls found the letters, paid for the postage, and forwarded them. The German finder enclosed a note of his own. (Please see pages. 196. 197, 202, 204, 206, 208.)

Later we received a postcard, also written in pencil and faded. It came from Auschwitz and it contained two coded messages that we struggled to comprehend at the time. Contrary to practice, she addressed our parents by their first names as though they were her friends. We understood that she would use certain camouflage for various reasons. She wanted her message to get through the Nazi censors, so she declared that "all is well, if you like, join me." But the other code we misunderstood totally. She said, "Against all my expectations I met your mother here and I see her every day." What did she mean? My parents' mothers had died long ago. We imagined that she may have met my mother's sister Pepi, who had been trapped and deported during the night raid in our neighborhood. If so, we thought, what joy they both must have felt at seeing one another. Only later, after the discovery of the death camps by the liberating Allied forces, did we understand what she meant. We then realized that she had tried to report that against all her expectations she had encountered death, and saw it every day. (See pages 10-11.)

You never discussed this realization with your parents.

I never brought up a topic that I felt would only torture us. Yet I knew they understood just as I did. They may have

The author with her mother, in the spring of 1944, in Brussels.

wrangled with the subject between themselves, but never in my presence. They always sought to protect me from hurt. When we received Herta's postcard, we hoped, we prayed, we thought she would survive. I often heard the Sonnenfelds and some of their friends, all Jews in hiding, say "we'll survive them," meaning our persecutors. The Allies were advancing and beating the Germans. We just needed to hold out until they liberated us.

Wasn't it surprising that the Nazis let any correspondence through at all?

They engaged in all kinds of tricks to fool everyone. Letting strictly-censored messages through once in a while was one of them. Of course, we too were misled, since we so much wanted to believe that with God's help, Herta would be all right.

Was your relationship with your parents always harmonious?

We were human, so of course we quarreled. Some disputes were also bitter. Although I was deeply hurt, I understood my mother's state of mind when during our disagreement she said that her best child was taken from her. I knew that my sister seemed to be the best of my parents' three children. I had observed her sweet nature, her kindness, her altruism and devotion. Still, such remarks were devastating. However, our closeness was genuine, it was our strength and hope, and we supported and counted on each other. Naturally, sometimes their frequent sadness and refusal to discuss the situation depressed and angered me. I wanted to have hope, even if it was only from day to day. My mother demanded understanding. "All my loved ones are gone," she would say reproachfully. Beyond these words she remained taciturn, she could say no more.

Did you ever hear from your brother during those years of persecution?

We received no communication from him. Naturally, we were anxious about his welfare, concerned about his health, his daily existence. Yet, relative to our distress about my sister, aunt, and cousins, we were optimistic regarding his safety. Somehow we trusted that he managed well in South America. We would hear from him after we survived the hellish nightmare. My mother often said, "God will help." We had to hold out, surmount the dangers, the anxieties, the boredom, and the lack of nourishment, both physical and mental.

Were you aware of the reasons for your mental malaise?

I knew that it was due to a deep discomfort with myself, the constant need to invent, to lie, to adapt to all circumstances and play various roles. How I envied the children described in my readings: children who were without ambivalence who had tranquil childhoods, who never had to run or hide; who grew up in ancestral houses where they could find material evidence of their ancestry in the attics; and who, by digging in chests and lockers, could discover photographs and letters belonging to former generations. How marvelous to define oneself by such a solid background!

I never discussed my reading with my big friend who lived on the floor below, or with her brother. I didn't know how to discuss a book. Not having had the experience, I thought it risky for fear that I it might show my lack of education. Such talk could be slippery ground where I might lack control, where, if put on the spot, I might again have to invent more lies. It was safer to speak about Simone's topics: ways to wear her hair, her clothes, her romances, her hopes for the future, her lack of freedom from her controlling mother. As for Pierre, he was an intelligent boy, but he was considered the baby and acted out the role imposed on him by his mother and his sister. Although I was only one year older, his family's attitude toward him influenced me, and thus I tended to regard him likewise. Simone offered me a view of an outside world. By then she had graduated from her *Ecole Professionnelle*. She had majored in *mode,* but instead of entering a career in fashion as contemplated during her school years, she became a government employee as a clerk in one of the *Ministères*. I never knew which one, perhaps because I paid little attention when she mentioned it. Later, it is likely that I did not inquire out of fear of displaying my ignorance of matters probably familiar to all Belgian citizens. She always referred to her place of work as *le ministère*. My attention to her stories flattered her, so that she enjoyed taking me along to local events. On holidays such as *Pentcôte* (Pentecost, or Whitsunday) I accompanied her and Pierre to fairs. Once in a while I even had some money and joined them in go cars and other rides. My parents let me go because they felt that since only the local rural residents attended these fairs, it was unlikely the Nazis had any interest in them. Regardless, they must have been quite anxious until I returned.

Also, I stayed out far beyond the curfew forced on Jews. We disregarded all restrictions placed on us by the Nazis. I had never worn the yellow star when it was first imposed, even on tiny toddlers. My father wore it for a while. However, just as did many other Jews, he hid it under a briefcase or a newspaper. Of course, soon the purpose of carrying such items under one's arm became quite obvious and dangerous. People ceased using camouflage, and stopped wearing the yellow star altogether. Sometimes Simone or one of her friends took me along to the center of town to see an afternoon performance of a musical revue. At such occasions I was very nervous, for this activity was a daring one. Many years later, as I thought about it, I concluded that I was often just plain lucky not to be caught. Still, this behavior was also a form of protection against being denounced by possible Nazi sympathizers. Once more, we gave the impression that our lives were no different from the rest of the population. We may have fooled some people. Whether or not we duped everyone, I can't say. As mentioned earlier (see page 113), I often worried whether Simone and her brother wondered why I never spoke about my teachers, my classmates, or the subjects I studied in the school that I supposedly attended. I managed to avoid those topics. When they came up in our conversations, I steered the focus away from me, and questioned either one of them. This scheme was successful, since they were always willing to speak of themselves. True, I was uneasy, but since I lacked an alternative, I suppressed the worry that nagged at me regarding their possible doubts. They probably suspected that I was hiding something.

But did you imagine they thought that you were Jewish?

I had reasons to believe that they didn't think so. On occasion Simone made derogatory remarks in my presence about Jews. I dismissed them because I realized that Jews were not liked in general. I often overheard people, some thoughtlessly, others without any real malice - at least so it seemed to me - use age old stereotypes to deride Jews. However, I knew that, had they been aware of who I really was, they wouldn't have verbalized those thoughts in my presence. The population was bombarded with anti-Semitic propaganda on billboards, in newspapers, and on the radio. Simone's mother pointed this out when my mother and I once visited shortly after we moved there. Noxious propaganda intermittently polluted the broadcasting of popular music. She dismissed it as ridiculous, yet the constant barrage may have infiltrated and left its residue. Simone's totally unrestrained and normal mannerism while entertaining anti-Semitic remarks in my presence, as well as in relating stories about Jews to me personally, reassured me of her ignorance concerning my background. Of course, I hated myself for my cowardice in failing to contradict her demeaning statements. Unfortunately, this sense of mortification about not revealing that I was Jewish remained with me, to my own sense of shame and self-hatred, for many decades to come.

My visits with Mme Maria, the landlady, and her daughter Clémentine, provided another escape from the deadly boredom. Their conversations opened for me a window on Flemish working class mores and customs: moral, cultural, and culinary.

Of course, it is only in retrospect that I recognize the all encompassing end product of those visits. I never thought of undertaking a sociological study. I never even knew the meaning or significance of the term. The stories I heard resembled my reading. Yet I found the vignettes that they recalled for me more interesting, since they were true-life descriptions and I knew the characters. Mme Maria reminisced about the wonderful dishes she had prepared at specific holidays when ingredients were plentiful. She spoke of her youth and her tribulations at work in sewing *ateliers*, and of her employers' sexual advances. She relished recalling her relationships with various admirers and their habits of propositioning her. She didn't characterize them as such, and I only faintly guessed at the meaning of her maxims. I clearly remember her words, *"Si un homme ne vous respecte pas la première fois qu'on sort avec lui, cet homme-là ne vaut rien."* (If a man does not respect you on the first date, such a man is worthless.) I did not wholly understand what was meant by "respect," and wondered why it seemed proper to be "respected" the first time and not subsequently as well. Yet I sensed that it was better not to question lest I appear stupid. As was the case with many of our conversations, I understood their content only many years later. Also, Mme Maria had no qualms in informing anyone that her daughter was born out of wedlock, that she was illegitimate. From my reading I knew what scandals such behavior caused in middle-class circles. Among Jews I had heard the derogatory Yiddish term *mamzer* (bastard) and recognized the terrible moral and social shame and condemnation that it expressed. I considered such an occurrence quite scandalous and marveled at the casualness of her remarks on the subject.

Their acquaintances had similar attitudes. One of them was the mother of little Annie. For a while Mme Maria took care of this sweet six-year-old girl, who was illegitimate as well. Her single mother, worked at two jobs: as a chambermaid at the Grand Hotel, and as a hairdresser's model. She wore her platinum hair coiffed in different ways each time she visited her daughter. At times she related shocking stories concerning her encounters with guests at the hotel, including some film stars. Mme Maria and Clémentine considered her pretentious because, even though she was Flemish, she insisted that her daughter attend a French speaking school. They often remarked, *"Hé bien, pour une femme de chambre . . . ! "* (Well, for a chamber maid. . . .!)

I liked Annie very much. She was affectionate and befriended me immediately. I enjoyed her laughing blue eyes and the way she shook her golden curls when dancing about the tile floor of the landlady's spacious kitchen. She loved to perform and recited over and again a poem that she had learned in her parochial school. Except for one line, I remember it all.

> *Le petit Jésus apprit à lire*
> *Dans la Bible aux longs perchemins,*
> *Que sa mère, avec un sourire*
> *. . . divins.*

> *Et le petit Jésus, de page en page*
> *Lisait de si bonne façon,*
> *Que sa mère à chaque leçon,*
> *Tendrement baisait l'enfant sage.*

> (Little Jesus learned to read
> In the long parchment of the Bible,
> That his mother, with a smile
> . . . . divine.

> And little Jesus, from page to page,
> Read so well,
> That his mother at each lesson,
> Tenderly kissed the good child.)

So, here was this little girl who constantly spoke of her experiences in school, and again I never mentioned any of mine to anyone.

As always, I hoped they paid no attention. However, in case they noticed, I prayed they would still believe that I attended school and that whatever the reason, my silence had to be respected. Since they never questioned me, for the sake of my peace of mind I wanted to assume that this was the case. Of course, I could never be sure and remained anxious.

A very nice neighbor frequently visited Madame Maria. I never knew our landlady's friend's real name because when speaking of her, she just referred to *la Walonne*, perhaps because Walloons (people of southern and southeastern Belgium whose language is French) were so rare in the area. *La Walonne*'s husband was a naturalized Belgian citizen who had lived in the country for many decades. Still, because he had been born in Rumania, Mme Maria and her daughter always referred to him as *le Roumain*. The couple had an only daughter about twenty years old, whose lack of participation in household chores was often the topic of the women's conversation.

Clémentine, the landlady's daughter, was among the first of the women hired as *receveuse*, on Brussels streetcars. Only men had formerly held such jobs. Now, such a position for a woman entailed great privilege and commanded a lot of respect in the two women's social standing. In her impressive uniform, Clémentine's job was to walk through the car, a heavy bag strapped to her shoulder that contained change and tickets attached to a metal plate. She sold fares and punched holes in long term-passes. When Clémentine returned from work, depending on her shift, I sometimes had the advantage of hearing the many stories of the frustration or amusement that she had experienced that day on her streetcar.

The long-standing animosity between Mme Maria and her next-door neighbor was another of my distractions. I never knew what had provoked their argument; their hostility seemed to flare up spontaneously. This often happened when they worked in the small open area of their respective gardens which were laid out side by side, and farther on, separated on either side by a white painted brick wall. When I heard the familiar loud shouting in Flemish, I ran to our rear window looking out on the gardens. Sometimes they accused one another of various petty crimes. The neighbor accused Mme Maria, among other vices, to have caused Mme Maria's husband's death. Our landlady retorted with her own accusations and insults. After ten minutes of shouting her lungs out, sometimes joined by her daughter, Mme Maria turned her back and retreated to her kitchen, all the while singing the first few lines of a popular French song:

> *Dans la vie faut pas s'en faire,*
> *Moi je'n m'en fais pas .*
> *De toutes ces p'tites misères*
> *Il ne faut pas s'en faire,*
> *Moi je'n m'en fais pas.*

> (In life one mustn't worry,
> I don't worry.
> About all these little miseries,
> One mustn't worry,
> I don't worry.)

And immediately from the neighbor came the reply in the form of another popular song:

> *Pourquoi mentir,*
> *Me mentir mon amour.*

> (Why do you lie,
> Lie to me my love.)

And so I coped with boredom as the days turned into weeks, then into months. Except for the weather, one season was similar to the next. Jewish festivals and holidays were forgotten; they came and went, and we did not notice. Faith was never the subject except for my mother's occasional wishful, *Gott wird helfen* (God will help). Our environment made us aware of Christian and national celebrations. We always presented our landlady with some gift on New Year's Day. Steadily I outgrew my clothes. My dresses and skirts were now embarrassingly short. The overcoat that Herta had made for me reached the middle of my thighs. Underwear and other clothing had turned to shreds. Food continued to be a daily preoccupation. The lack of proper nutrition manifested itself when the slightest scratch or small burn became infected and did not heal.

Time crept on, until one day we heard that the Allies had landed in Normandy. Our hopes soared while anxiously we waited. Some people listened to the forbidden broadcast of the BBC relating the Allies' terrible battles against the German army. Then we heard of the enemy's crumbling resistance. The Allies were advancing! When Paris was liberated, our confidence swelled. Still we remained cautious lest our optimism land us in an enemy trap. Soon convoys of German troops were rumbling in retreat through the city's streets. As days went by, the columns diminished to single trucks spotted here and there. Eventually, bicycles were the Germans' sole recourse, until finally they fled on foot heading east, weary and unkept - sometimes in small groups or pairs, often alone.

CHAPTER VII

LIBERATION

Liberation came to Brussels on September 4, 1944. Allied tanks, armored personnel carriers, and those strange-looking automobiles never seen before called jeeps , rolled through the thoroughfares of our suburb of Anderlecht. How did I get to that intersection to watch that marvelous sight of the incoming liberators? I probably heard on the street where to go and then followed the crowd. I was there all by myself in the throng of cheering people on that glorious sunny day, totally transported, overcome with wonder and happiness. It was all so unbelievable, this feeling of elation, this surge of exultation! No more fear, we were liberated, we really had survived! British troops manned the first convoys. People climbed onto the vehicles, and embraced and kissed the smiling young soldiers. How we blessed them, how we loved them! The following day when my three older friends went into town, I joined them, as I had many times before under the previously grim circumstances. But this time I went with a totally new sensation. I discovered that wondrous freedom from all apprehension, that amazing feeling of release from trepidation. Young people, cheering and singing, hung from the platforms of jammed streetcars. The city was packed as though all the inhabitants, full of mirth and animation, had converged in its center. The people of Brussels were delirious with happiness, dancing, singing, and celebrating every Allied soldier in sight. We had our picture taken in the street; first Simone and Solange, then Henriette and I, walking down Boulevard Adolphe Max, each of us, arms linked, flanking a British soldier.

In the weeks that followed the Liberation, the euphoria settled down, leaving us simply in high spirits. I remember the inner joy of walking the streets without anxiety. This new sensation made us that much more conscious of the overwhelming fear we had endured. But now, instead of the horrid Nazi flags, glorious Allied flags hung from buildings: Belgian, French, British, American, Soviet. Posters in shop windows, and on kiosk walls shouted in huge bold colors and letters, *"On les a eus!"* (We got them!). Street singers played a new song, and everyone sang along,

> *Ils sont foutus, on les reverra plus.*
> *Les Fridolins sont partis pour Berlin.*

(They are done for, we'll not see them again.
The Fritzes have gone to Berlin.)

Allied soldiers filled the city. The Americans were especially in evidence because of their habit of sitting on the steps of public buildings. Amazed and amused, we observed how they covered the steps of the Bourse (stock exchange) as if in an amphitheater, sitting there relaxed while they watched the street scene.

Now that you could circulate freely, did you see any of the Jewish children you had known before going into hiding?

The only one was Fredi a boy with the same first name as my deported cousin, and whose last name I cannot remember. I met this former playmate when walking one Sunday afternoon in the center of Brussels with my parents. Fredi was accompanied by his mother who had been widowed for many years, and his aunt. They were acquaintances from the time of the *Comité*. The other Jewish children I had known in the old neighborhood and from school had vanished. Here and there we encountered a few people whom we knew by sight. Some whom I had never seen recognized me from having seen me on stage. How distant those days seemed then. Yet, I was pleased and very surprised to find I had been so well known that the remnants of the community still recognized me.

The fortunate Jews who had been lucky enough to elude the traps of the Nazis emerged from their hiding places. The ones who had been well off came to claim their belongings that had been left with gentiles for safekeeping. I was present when Henriette spoke to Simone about Solange, who no longer had her attractive *chamberlain*. This was the name given to tall umbrellas that were in fashion, named after the former British prime minister who, when seen in newsreels, always carried a tall umbrella. The fact that her *chamberlain* belonged to Jews was the reason for Solange's sudden dispossession. A Jewish family had left their belongings in Solange's parents' care before going into hiding, and the umbrella was among the items claimed. She hated to give it up, and from Henriette's report I gathered that Solange's family didn't feel very kindly toward these reemerging Jews. *"Les Juifs sont revenus "* (the Jews have returned) was the saying.

I wasn't upset that my friend and her family harbored such ill feelings. Their sentiments did not in the least surprise me. This was the world I knew; I dismissed the incident, considering it expected, not in the least unsual. It confirmed again that Jews were unpopular, and if they enjoyed material ease, they were especially envied and resented. Also, I understood Solange's pique at having to give up the *chamberlain* that for two years she had considered her own.

Therefore, I continued to keep my origins secret and persisted in maintaining a double life and preserving a double personality. I rationalized that the war was going to end soon and then, one way or another, we would leave Belgium for the United States, where I would start anew. The people to whom I lied would no longer be part of my life. But in the meantime I would go on as before because I knew that a confession on my part would earn me their contempt. We still lived in their proximity since our material situation remained unchanged. Although we no longer feared being deported, we continued struggling for food, fuel, clothing, and shelter. I had no doubt of their condemnation and found it justifiable. After all, I had deceived them, even abused their confidence. Besides, since I knew that Jews were not liked, my admission would only confirm the stereotypical image. In addition, I had become accustomed to this persona. To reveal the fiction would destroy a part of myself that I was still unable to discard. It had served me as a shelter from danger and hurt. I could not admit to anyone that I was Jewish, except sometimes to other Jews.

But when you were finally able to enroll in school, you told the registrar. How did this admission come about?

With the Nazis gone, school was now open to everyone. Yet, I did not know where to go or what to do. After missing two years, how could I catch up, leaping over what seemed an educational chasm between the "normal" students and myself? My parents could not advise me. I was on my own in my search, groping for ways to integrate into a student body. Then I thought of the possibility of enrolling in that professional school that my three older friends had attended. I had heard all about it from them for such a long time. So why not try; after all, it had supplied these girls with good training. It offered a choice of disciplines for the working world in business and trades, while providing at the same time a general education. Besides, it was well located; although most students took the streetcar, the school was still within walking distance for me.

The registrar inquired as to why I had not attended school all this time. I had not anticipated these questions; they took me totally by surprise, and I was mortified. I broke down and cried as I answered, ashamed of having to admit my situation, degraded, feeling guilty in the role of the victim. Of course I should have been prepared for her questions; they made sense. Still I wasn't, primarily because I expected to develop a normal existence now that I was able to return to school. In that process, I anticipated putting aside all the mental anguish I had experienced. Instead, I was confronted with admitting a reality that I had constantly sought to evade and forget. The residue of this experience remained with me for decades, and since I sought to avoid any such reoccurrences, I always dodged the questions. When avoiding them was impossible, I lied.

Unfortunately, counseling was not available at the school, or I would not have chosen a program so unsuitable to my abilities and taste. I don't know whether or not counseling was ever practiced at that time in Belgian schools. The fact remains that the woman reassured me quickly that all students were now accepted, and she enrolled me forthwith in the program I had requested, perhaps to soothe my feelings, as she was touched by my grief, and maybe embarrassed that her questions caused such misery. Although she timidly put forth the advisability of my pursuing more ambitious endeavors, her feeble attempt and manner in voicing that proposition failed to persuade me, as I was convinced of my handicap. Therefore, I never investigated the other possibilities that the school offered. Indeed, the program I chose proved unsatisfactory. I was unchallenged and bored. I had no affinity with my classmates, who came from a background similar to that of the girls at the convent school. The only experience I enjoyed there was my introduction to English, an excellent course that the other girls in my program didn't attend. I befriended one girl whose father was a streetcar conductor. Just as it was for Clémentine, his uniform commanded respect and admiration in the neighborhood. My friend was an only child, and I found the parents' protectiveness of their daughter very touching and admirable. It seemed so strange because my attitude toward my own parents mirrored theirs toward her. Our friendship, however, remained superficial because other than some personal affinity, we really had little in common.

I soon left the school in search of different ways to leapfrog over what seemed to me at the time an educational abyss.

My constant concern to overcome the gap in my education inhibited my search for an appropriate educational framework. Eventually I discovered an institution with an interesting curriculum where I found affinity with the subjects offered and with my fellow students. Nevertheless, filling the cracks remained an ongoing process throughout my adolescence and into adulthood.

In the meantime, following liberation, we experienced the coldest, most severe winter we had ever known. I have no recollection of deep snow, what stands out most is the penetrating cold of the rooms because of the scarcity of fuel, the icy streets, and the gray skies. Our threadbare clothes offered scant protection. I especially recall the numbness in my feet. Although we had been liberated, resources were difficult to come by, and we endured severe material hardship. Furthermore, besides being continually anguished by not knowing the whereabouts of our loved ones, that winter my father contracted pneumonia and fell gravely ill. At the time, both of my parents worked in a furrier workshop. After my father became ill, only my mother could work. She sometimes brought wood or coal home with her when she returned at night. My father recovered after a long and painfully slow convalescence.

The war kept on going. Soon the news spread of a German counteroffensive in the Ardennes led by a general named von Rundstedt. Everyone learned that name very quickly. We were terrified that the Nazis might return. Heavy-hearted and dismayed, we heard of the Allies' heavy losses. In addition, the Germans subjected us now to rocket raids, at any time of night or day. The night raids stand out clearly in my mind, as sirens wailed the arrival of the first V-I rocket. We heard its oncoming rumble, comparable to the sound of a malfunctioning motor; louder and louder the noise grew, and when it stopped abruptly, the rocket fell right then and there, regardless of the site. There was no safe area from these rockets, they fell by chance, indiscriminately, terrifying the population. I recall waking up in horror at the sound of the fearful sirens and hearing just minutes later the dreaded hacking of the rocket. Terrified as it grew louder, I anticipated that its clatter would stop right above our house, that it would fall on us and explode. As it passed, the sound grew dimmer, and the tension in my body abated. However, now my imagination followed the cursed missile, listening, pitying and fearing for its victims. Then at a later time there followed the V-2 rocket, when the alerting sirens no longer served much purpose, since the rockets' speed prevented the spotters from locating them soon enough. By the time they came into view, they were nearly upon us and about to crash. Promptly we learned to distinguish the V-l from the V-2 by their separate sounds. Both rockets were dreaded, but the V-2 with its more powerful and wider range of destruction, amplified the havoc and the consternation. Some missiles fell in fields or other unpopulated areas, but many dropped on thickly settled sections of the city. Newspapers photos showed the grim effects of their devastation.

Still, all the mental anguish engendered by the rockets, the reports of the success of the German counteroffensive and Allied losses, the material woes, and the physical discomfort, pale in comparison to what followed that winter's setbacks. The memories of the events that ensued are the most painful for me to recall. With the welcome news of the Allied armies' repulse of the German counteroffensive, and the gradual relief from the cold weather, there appeared a new foreboding and alarming phenomenon. Nature's renewal presented a total contrast to the havoc of our state of mind and heart. Horribly emaciated, skeleton like survivors of the death and concentration camps who had been liberated by the advancing Allied forces, arrived on the scene, some of them still clothed in the horrid striped inmate garb. From them we learned firsthand what had occurred in those camps; what unimaginable torture they had undergone. We learned of the unspeakable extent of the killings, the gassings! The overwhelming horror at these descriptions left us in shock, numb with pain. They said that it was worse than anything imaginable, that the terror was indescribable. The survivors wanted to tell of their experiences, but I could no longer bear to listen. The thought of my sweet sister, my aunt, my cousins, in those circumstances drove me insane. Most of all I feared for my mother; I wanted to protect her, shield her from the torture of the overpowering horror. Of course their accounts were impossible to conceive. How could anyone, even the Nazis, inflict such unimaginable suffering on other human beings! However, the survivors' stories were soon confirmed when in the movie houses, preceding the featured film, newsreels showed the scenes that Allied soldiers encountered as they discovered the camps. My mother's pain, her bone-chilling, prolonged moaning was more than I could bear. I pleaded with her, beseeched her not to watch. Yet I could not tell whether I convinced her with my imploring, for I averted my own eyes from the screen, and holding her close with both arms, I lowered my head onto her shoulder. Yet, somehow I sensed that she kept watching as though riveted to the sight of the exposed horror.

I have pushed these recollections into the furthest recesses of my mind. Throughout my adolescence and adulthood, I kept the memory of my lost childhood in the darkest of shadows. But I have veiled these particular events of my life much more than any other. Indeed, to recall this very episode is by far the most difficult, the most upsetting. Only with strong determination and volition can I summon up the fortitude to break through these shadows, to tear the veils, to visualize again in memory these scenes, and to verbalize in written words the heartbreak of these situations. Words fail, adjectives are inadequate, they underrate the depth of the distress and sorrow of the experience.

Where did you encounter the survivors?

Mostly at newly set up Jewish service agencies, where we searched through lists of survivors. There my mother, holding my sister's picture in her hand, ran from one survivor to another asking in her trembling voice whether he or she had seen my sister. Each one looked but shook his or her head.

The overwhelming grief in her face, in her total demeanor, was unbearable. Her wide, dry eyes evoked her excruciating pain more than if she had had the capacity to weep. She could no longer cry. Powerless, I followed her as she criss-crossed the rooms each time she spotted a different survivor. Day after day we came to inquire whether new lists had arrived. Anxiously we examined them, praying that somehow we would find a beloved name. Day after day we returned, but each time the search proved futile. Yet, we continued to search, praying that the next day, or the day after, we would spot their names on a new list of survivors.

I never gave up hope that we would find my sister. At the time we still didn't know how very few had escaped the killings. Many of the survivors whom we met originated from other parts of Europe; only some were from Belgium. So I trusted, and prayed that some day she too would return, or that somewhere, perhaps in a different country, somehow we would find her. Yet our mood was desolate. Each day watching my parents' distress brought renewed heartache. My memories of the time are clouded in gray, even though supposedly there was sunshine outside.

I recall our dim rooms in accordance with our state of soul on the day that a friendly policeman, in charge of conducting some kind of survey, came to call on us. He sat at our table filling out forms, asking questions of my mother and me. My father was not there. Noticing our sad demeanor, this nice man, looking out from beneath his white helmet, offered words of consolation. He addressed my mother and asked me to translate. We appreciated his intentions, but his words which were made up of generalities and platitudes, brought little comfort. The last sentence of his short speech stands out sharply in my mind. He said, ". . . we all did ("all" included us) our best, and what was required for *la patrie* (the fatherland)." Contrary to his motives, his words evoked in me only feelings of sadness, a profound sense of irony and isolation. How could we be included in the symbolism of the word *patrie*? With our lives bereft of loved ones, deprived of stability, we were still stateless refugees, always outsiders of some kind or another. I envied his sense of *patrie* and wished that it really could include us. I nodded appreciatively and said I would tell my mother. I recall distinctively not telling her, because I knew that his words held no meaning for us. My mother's expression indicated that she understood the man's good intentions from his tone of voice and demeanor. Nevertheless, she never asked me to translate exactly what he said. This was an example, as it happened sometimes, of a situation in which speech was superfluous between us, in which the feeling was transmitted and understood. I sensed that the policeman recognized the futility of his endeavor in our situation. His manner and expression indicated his thoughts; he had tried his best, and so he resumed filling out his forms.

Meanwhile, given our ceaseless financial destitution, we availed ourselves of the assistance of a Jewish agency that had set up a canteen providing lunch, the principal meal of the day. I recall going mainly with my mother. The facility was located in a part of the city requiring, what seemed to me then, a fairly long ride on the streetcar. I remember depressing long tables with benches on either side. The day we ate sardines stands out in my memory; such a treat we had not tasted in years. Since the predicament of so many Jews paralleled our own, we encountered there a wide range of social and intellectual levels among the diners, all happy to partake of this sustenance. However, after a time I refused to return; I found the place depressing and our situation demeaning. I preferred going without. Some of the people I saw at the canteen upset me by their attitude and their appearance, so that after a while I disliked returning. Yet, one specific incident triggered the end of my partaking there. It was the conduct of two young men facing us across the table. They overheard our conversation and every so often broke in to add remarks. When my mother incidentally commented that I needed to hasten to school, one of them laughingly interjected a well-known maxim in German, saying that if I hadn't learned enough by now, I wouldn't do so in the future either. Instead of showing contempt, my mother seemed amused. Although irritated and saddened, I some-how understood that the cause of her amusement was mainly this German maxim that she had not heard for some time. The young men's rude mannerisms and clownish comments offended me that much more because they reminded me of the comments I had overheard our landlady make to her friends on my account. She considered studying a luxury practiced only by the well-to-do, by people who could afford not to work. In her social class, studying was not considered work. She thought that working was using one's hands and that a young girl of already fourteen should work so as to contribute to household expenses. In my state of insecurity, such comments only enhanced my feelings of culpability and self-doubt. I pretended to ignore the young man's remarks, but they affected me sufficiently to put an end to any further visits to the canteen.

In the midst of catching up, or rather skipping over the gaps in my education left from my years in hiding, I found a learning environment more to my liking. I never fully over-came the inner, looming presence of this breach. Yet, I took great care in masking my feelings of inadequacy from my teachers and classmates. I finally enrolled in a business in-stitute. There I learned typing, business French and Flem-ish, as well as shorthand in both languages. Later I resumed studying English, added Spanish, and German writing and syntax.

It is surprising that you chose to study German. Some years later you could not bear to hear or speak this language.

Memory and consciousness need time and maturity to de-velop. The full impact of the horror implanted itself gradu-ally as time elapsed. Besides, I always communicated in Ger-man with my parents and their acquaintances. I considered practical aspects; since my speech was fluent, I thought it a pity not to be completely literate. Moreover, I studied En-glish, expecting that some day our dream of going to the United States would be realized. As for Spanish, beside its possible use in the future, my interest was also connected to the fact that my brother Ernst lived in a Spanish-speaking country where some day I hoped to travel. I liked languages and learned them with ease. Also, a person who was proficient in several languages enjoyed much prestige, and I contemplated a career either in export-import or in multilingual translation.

Had you already heard from Ernst by then?

We already knew that he had made his way to Argentina from Bolivia where he had landed originally. However, we had not been able to communicate with him for the past two years. All the while, although grateful that he had succeeded in evading the Nazis' clutches by leaving Europe, my parents agonized about his well-being. We assumed that life was difficult for him, and that assumption proved to be correct. By the time we heard from him, his situation had improved considerably. I cannot recall whether his first letter reached us after Liberation or after May 1945, once the war was over in Europe.

In search of a better livelihood, my parents started a partnership with Martin Wasserman, my father's former coworker and close acquaintance from our mutual hiding place in the uniform factory. He and his wife had fled Germany and were fellow refugees. Both were middle-aged, tall and slender, cultured and distinguished. They were childless. He had been a fine furrier in Leipzig, she an actress on the classic German stage. My parents and Wasserman obtained contracts from the British army, at the time a large presence in Belgium. This was when both my parents worked in a furrier workshop as previously mentioned (see page 152), making small stuffed dogs out of rabbit fur. Because of the war, Britain had stopped making toys but arranged for their manufacture abroad. The Wassermans lived close to the center of Brussels in a rented ground floor apartment, and a workshop was set up in the basement of their building. My parents were happy to have sustenance. Sadly, continually working with pelts was to have future repercussions on my father's health.

Stephie Wasserman, then in her late forties or early fifties, continued to perform now and then for the Jewish-German-Austrian refugee community in Brussels. Occasionally I participated in these performances, but, to my parents' chagrin, I no longer directed my efforts toward a future on the stage, instead hoping to use my facility with foreign languages, most likely in some commercial enterprise.

All the while I kept on feeling responsible for my parents' well-being and happiness. The responsibility entrusted to me by my sister in her letter never left me. But because of my separate endeavors at that time, our course of interests diverged somewhat.

Were they still searching for Herta and the others?

On their own, my parents continued looking for additional lists of survivors. I was unaware of what other inquiries they undertook. I realized only much later that at the time, the Wassermans assisted and supported my parents with advice in their search for our loved ones. Only long after did I realize that my parents had kept this additional search from me. They tried to spare me as my interests and life little by little separated from theirs. As in the past, my level of anxiety kept rising and falling according to their state of mind. Burdened by the heavy hearts around me, I sought optimistic surroundings with normal children free from care and sadness.

And so, did you secure good friendships at the commerce and language schools?

I met several nice girls, four in particular whom I liked very much. Unfortunately, our relationship could not develop since to my chagrin, I soon discovered that one of them was an ardent anti-Semite who very quickly influenced the other three.

Had you revealed your true identity, could you have influenced their thinking?

I had no such hope. At fourteen I lacked the maturity as well as the necessary courage to engage in an argument on the subject. I was conditioned by years of silence and denial. Also, I felt powerless, ignorant of effective ways to persuade, yet all the while hating myself for my inability and for what I considered cowardice. Still, I was convinced that the anti-Semite's mind was made up. I knew she would prevail in her prejudices no matter what I said to her. She brought her persuasions both from her home environment and from her nineteen-year-old Polish soldier friend, who was serving in the Polish Brigade, a division of the British army. She often quoted his remarks: *"Tout ce qui se passe en Pologne, c'est la faute des Juifs."* (All that is happening in Poland is the Jews' fault.)

At the time I was also affected by several other disheartening encounters, reinforcing my persistence in hiding my true identity. I met a number of persons, during common occurrences, who kept blaming Jews for whatever difficulties they experienced. While waiting at a streetcar stop, a seemingly nice, well-dressed woman engaged another passenger and me in conversation. She complained of high taxes and blamed the Minister of Finance, a Jew. Oh yes, she said, do you see how all the Jews who reappeared and retuned have money? Well, that's because Gutt is a Jew.[27] The subject arose also in my Spanish language class. When I attempted to come to the Jews' defense, trying to induce sympathy by arguing that this persecuted people had just suffered so horrendously. The two young adults in the class not only thwarted my attempts immediately by arguing against me but also tried to persuade me, warning me not to be duped. In addition, the teacher agreed with them. I remained dumbfounded, totally incredulous that these people with whom I had felt such affinity, also turned out to be anti-Semites.

Of course, if you had been frank about your identity, you probably would not have suffered such disenchantments. Those remarks would not have been made in your presence.

That is easy to say in retrospect. On the other hand, had I been candid, the hurt would very well have taken on different aspects, leaving me disillusioned just the same. At the time I wanted to merge with people who did not suffer. It took time for me to realize the futility of such attempts and the detriment to myself.

So you searched for other social contacts. How did you learn of the Jewish Austrian youth group?

Most probably in one of the café concert, cabarets, or other theater performances arranged by some of their enterprising dilettante stage managers. As was the case before the German invasion, after the Liberation a multitude of such enterprises sprung up. I often joined my parents in attending some such performances. Sometimes I also took a part in them, but finally refused to participate regardless of my parents' regret. On occasion we met there soldiers of the Jewish Brigade from the then Palestinian division of the British army. Everyone was filled with pride and gratitude at the sight of these young men. The war was still going on, and we mourned the Allies' many casualties. Newscasts and newspapers reported on how their armies defeated the enemy on all fronts. This news boosted our hopes for our loved ones, and we prayed that more people would be liberated as the Allies advanced. We speculated that once the war ended, our loved ones would return from wherever they were.

The Austrian youth group was part of a larger organization of people who had fled Nazi Austria. It was housed in a rented three-story building in a residential neighborhood of Brussels. The office, located on the ground floor, was staffed by a young woman in her late teens or early twenties, who often participated in the young peoples' activities. The age of the group members ranged from thirteen to the late twenties. Friendships developed separately among the younger and the older members whose social contacts expanded outside the group. But a warm affinity extended throughout, regardless of age. We met weekly in the rented house, most often on Sundays. We talked, sang, danced, went on outings and on retreats. I felt comfortable, as I was reminded of the social occasions sponsored by the *Comité* of old. The young teenagers, having grown up in Brussels, spoke French among themselves. I enjoyed the singing of the old Viennese ballads, folk songs and hiking songs that my mother and sister so often sang together. Some of the older members were survivors of death camps. Some members' parents had been deported. They too kept consulting lists of survivors, hoping to find their loved ones' names. One boy in such a predicament also had a sister, who, having been placed in hiding in a convent and been converted, insisted on remaining there. Moreover, she planned to enter the religious order. This young man waited for his parents' return, when he hoped they would persuade their daughter to leave the convent. Nelli, who at one time headed the group, was about eighteen or nineteen. She too was waiting for her parents and often encouraged mine not to despair, saying that my sister too would come back. After all, she told them, why should they not keep hoping when she herself refused to give up hope.

May 7, 1945, started as a glorious day in every respect. The warm and bright spring sunshine reinforced the symbolic value of the end of the war in Europe. Once more, the city was in an uproar with glee, and the jubilation was almost as buoyant as on the day of Liberation. Church bells rang out, people danced and sang in the streets.

As previously agreed with my parents, I left my friends amid all the celebration to join them later that afternoon at the Wassermans' home. Animated with the happiness I had experienced with my friends and the people in the streets, I fully expected to continue celebrating and sharing the joy with my parents and their friends. However, immediately upon entering their living room my spirits sank. To my amazement I found my parents in the deepest state of depression. When my queries were left unanswered I verbalized my impatience and resentment. With very subdued demeanor our friends tried to intervene, counseling indulgence on my part. But my vitality was drained, and so, rather than suppress my feelings of disappointment, I pitied myself and said that I found my parents' pessimism excessive.

The war had ended, why despair today of all days when hope should triumph! Still they remained frozen in sadness.

What was to have been a most wonderful day, marking the war's end, has remained one of the most painful memories of my life. The contradiction between the joy experienced outside in the street and the unexplained, deepened distress permeating that room left an indelible imprint on my spirit. My parents' refusal to explain the increase of their mental pain left me bitter and bewildered.

Had I been more mature, and perhaps more astute, I would have recognized many signs. For example, I would have pressed my sister's girlhood friend Walter, who had survived and come back, for more information. When I spoke to him of our waiting for my sister's return, he said, *"Tote können nicht aufstehen"* (the dead cannot rise). I dismissed his remark, thinking to myself, "What does he know, he has no proof !" Still, I dropped the subject and never inquired of him as to how he could make such a statement. I assumed that he suspected the worst because so far we had not heard from her. My refusal to give up hope resulted in obtuseness. Or rather, I kept living in perpetual denial. Only several decades later did I realize that on that very day of the end of the war my parents had learned that my sister, my aunt, and my two cousins had perished.[28] At the time I did not realize that it was not only the lists of survivors that were available, but also the lists of those who had died. Of course I never imagined that my parents would keep the truth from me. However, since they wanted to spare me, they did not tell me. I assume that they thought that with the passage of time I would slowly come to understand what had transpired, since neither my sister, nor any of the others were coming back. They expected that by then, time would have dulled the pain. What they didn't realize was that I kept on hoping for decades. My sister was missing, but someday she would be found. As years passed, I often thought she might be lost somewhere, wandering about Eastern Europe, perhaps in some Russian camp suffering from amnesia. I struggled with feelings of culpability for my lack of courage to go looking for her in some way or other in that part of Europe, in displaced persons camps that I had seen in newsreels. As time went on, indeed I came to assume that since neither my sister nor any of our other relatives had returned, the inevitable had to be accepted. However, the nagging doubt and guilt feeling of not having gone in search of my sister lingered deep in my consciousness. These feelings were reinforced when I returned to Europe from the United States twelve years later with my infant daughter and my husband, who was entering a two-year post doctoral fellowship at Oxford University. I had never been to England before, and in many ways, I felt far removed there from that continent where all our hardship had occurred. Nevertheless, I had returned to that part of the world and was tortured by my cowardice, for I thought that now I ought to have the courage to go in search of my sister.

It was only accidentally that I came to realize that my parents had indeed received confirmation of my sister's death. Again, this happened many years later when my two children were already of grammar school age. I was typing a letter to my father's lawyer. The atmosphere was fraught with emotion inasmuch as the subject matter was my sister. As my father dictated to me, his eyes were red and filled with tears. He stipulated that he had been deprived of a daughter because she perished in a Nazi death camp. Skeptical, I looked up at him and remarked that he could not uphold such a statement seeing that he never had received any real confirmation of the fact. My father's expression was one of extreme surprise. At once I realized that he had totally forgotten that I had never been told. Like a flash, the day that marked for me the end of the war resurfaced in my mind. For an instant I relived the scene and the pain of that afternoon. I knew then that on that very day, my parents had received the dreadful confirmation.

Fearful of emotional stress in excavating painful memories, I resumed typing without any further questions. I thought, "Better let the past stay buried, what use was there in torturing ourselves by dwelling on this horrid episode of our lives?"

In retrospect, I am not so sure that those were my father's sentiments as well. He may have wanted to speak about the past, but both of my parents sensed my reluctance and never raised the subject. Unfortunately, they are gone now, so I will never know.

RETURN TO BRUSSELS

The first gathering of former hidden children in New York City, in May 1991, brought forth in me an unsettling imposition: to retrieve those memories out of the shadows where they had dwelled for many decades still vivid, but veiled and curtained off. I have struggled to lift the veiling layers resulting in the recollections described in this book.

Many endeavors followed this first conference. In the summer of 1993 a gathering convened in Jerusalem, and another in Montreal in October 1994. I had the privilege to participate in both. *L'Enfant Caché de Belgique* (The Hidden Child of Belgium) is one of the organizations among the many that emerged from the first conference in New York. This same association announced at the Montreal meeting a forthcoming conference of former hidden children from Belgium, France, and Holland, to be held in Brussels in the spring of 1995. I decided that I would attend. I expected that, among other things, it would give me the opportunity to learn from other people who had been hidden in Belgium, as well as to assemble confirmation of events during the Nazi occupation. In addition, I would seek out the Catholic boarding and day school that played such an important part in the psychological landscape of my childhood. At last I would assure myself of its name, which as mentioned previously, remained completely erased from my mind. I would also try to collect some information about my Jewish classmate Louise. In addition, I planned to muster up the courage to look for the house in which we hid in the basement during that Nazi night raid of the neighborhood. My husband would accompany me and lend me moral support. We anticipated attending the two-day conference and further to spend another eleven days in Brussels to allow time to gather the needed information.

I had returned to Brussels before on several occasions for professional meetings or when in transit to other destinations in Europe. However, I always went to parts of the city that had no connection with my unhappy past. As the date of departure approached, panic set in. Why was I doing this to myself? Why return, why search for places where I had been miserable? Of course, I knew I would go, I was committed psychologically, just as I had imposed on myself the writing of this memoir. I thought that going back to Brussels to attend this meeting was a proper way to come full circle. In spite of my reasoning, I struggled with anxiety.

The panic abated somewhat in the plane. Upon arrival in Brussels we took a taxi through areas unfamiliar to me, and the location of our hotel, though familiar, was also benign. The conference itself was to be held at the *Université Libre de Bruxelles,* known as the bastion of freedom, liberal thought, and fairness.[29] These very aspects of the environment, mental and physical, alleviated my misgivings.

As at previous conferences, the bond between people who spent their childhood in hiding from Nazi persecution was immediate. Yet this time I felt that the solidarity was even more powerful, no doubt because of shared geographical ties. As in previous meetings, this was especially noticeable in the small workshops where we discussed our experiences. Locations, and addresses where people had searched lists in the hope of finding their loved ones were mentioned. *Place Rouppe,* yes of course, that was where the Jewish agency had been located; that was the name of the square that I couldn't remember, where we had pored over the lists of survivors. Between plenary sessions I visited the book display, where I knew I would find the *Mémorial de la Déportation des Juifs de Belgique,* a large volume consisting, among other details, of all the names of the Jews deported from Belgium who perished in the death camps, compiled by Serge Klarsfeld and Maxime Steinberg. The authors had retrieved the meticulous records that the Germans had kept. This book was already available for examination at the first conference in New York in 1991, but I had avoided consulting it then. At the time I could not bear the thought of finding the names of my loved ones listed among the murdered victims. This time I fought to overcome my anguish, and I searched for them. And for the first time in my life, I encountered the actual confirmation of their deaths. The renewed feeling of sorrow was devastating as I found what I expected. Indeed, they were all there: my sister, her husband, my aunt, my two cousins. Listed as well were the dates and numbers of the transports that took them from the assembly camp of the old Caserne Dossin, the antechamber of death in Malines, to Auschwitz.

I saw that my then seventeen-year-old cousin Fred Dermer left with the first convoy for Auschwitz from the Malines assembly camp on August 4, 1942. The first transport deported 998 persons, among them 140 children less than sixteen years of age. Upon arrival, 254 people were gassed. On May 8, 1945, seven remained alive out of the 998.[30]

My aunt Pepi Dermer, née Kohn, was deported from Malines with the XIth convoy September 26, 1942. Among the 1,742 persons were 523 children. Eighty percent of the people of this convoy were gassed upon arrival at Auschwitz. Of the total deported by this transport, thirty survivors remained on May 8, 1945.[31]

My brother-in-law, Israel Krygier, first sent to the north of France and put to work along the coast of the English channel[32] was ultimately shipped to Malines. He is listed in convoy XVII of October 31, 1942, from Malines. My sister Herta, was caught in Brussels four months after her husband was sent to the north of France. Herta was deported in convoy

XIV on October 24, 1942,[33] only seven days before her husband's arrival in Malines. They could not have seen one another because the deportees of the convoy of October 31, 1942, consisting mainly of men coming from camps of the organization Todt in northern France, were kept on the train and never entered the Caserne Dossin. However, 148 of them jumped from the train before it crossed the Belgian border. But 919 of them, exhausted and weakened by their experience in northern France, were gassed upon arrival at Auschwitz.[34]

My cousin Max Glasz was deported from Malines in convoy XX, on April 20, 1943, two days after his twenty-eighth birthday. Among the 1,631 deportees, the oldest of whom was ninety-one, were 262 children, the youngest of whom was thirty-nine days old. Two hundred and thirty-one deportees jumped from the moving train, but twenty were killed by German bullets. Upon arrival at Auschwitz, 63 percent of the remaining fourteen hundred deportees were gassed.[35]

Dejected, I paid for the book and slid it into my briefcase to conceal it from my own view among the many brochures, books, and papers connected with the conference. All the while I was conscious of its heavy presence and feeling, held next to my body, its bulk and its content. On our way to our separate workshops, my husband, knowing my pain, offered to carry the book, which I gratefully accepted.

The latter part of the afternoon of the first day was devoted to honoring the righteous gentiles who saved the lives of Jewish children by hiding them in their midst. Thanks to their courage and generosity, the lives of five thousand Jewish children were saved. In cases in which the people in question were no longer alive, their offspring or other relatives received the medals in their stead. Among the recipients were several retired nuns. More than seven hundred persons attended the conference, and that afternoon the large amphitheater was filled. We mounted the steps to an upper row where we spotted two seats available next to the already occupied aisle seat. I apologized for troubling the woman who stood up to let us through. As I weaved past her and turned to sit down, she excitedly grabbed me, kissed me, all the while calling over and over, Inge Scheer, Inge Scheer! I was dumbfounded to hear this name that I hadn't been called by since childhood. It was my maiden name combined with my former first name. I had long disliked and rejected it, for beside the pain that it recalled, no Belgian had been able to pronounce "Inge" properly, and it had made me stand out immediately as a foreigner. As mentioned in Chapter V (page 110,) I had discarded it in 1942 when, going into hiding, I sought to blend in with the local population and at that time I changed it to Irène. Hearing someone call me Inge, brought forth deep discomfort because that name symbolized for me years of profound unhappiness. Now, all of a sudden it seemed to emerge from some distant depth, ringing totally alien from my evolved persona five decades later. Bewildered, we stared at each other. She spoke her own former name: Edith Berger! For the moment it meant nothing to me. I recognized neither her face nor her name. How did she know me, how could she recognize me? Then she reminded me that her sister had been my classmate. Both our families had fled Austria, and as refugees we became acquainted in Brussels. Together we had played hopscotch and jump rope. After going into hiding in 1942, we lost sight of each other. Suddenly, fifty-three years later, here we were meeting again by mere chance. I was stunned. Knowing that most of my Jewish playmates and classmates had been deported, I never expected to see again anyone I had known as a child.

All around us our encounter had created excitement. Sympathetic people listened eagerly, questioned us enthusiastically. Edith explained that she and her three siblings had survived in hiding. Her parents had been caught and deported. Her father had perished, and her mother had suffered medical experimentations in the death camp. Miraculously she had survived and returned, although in poor health.

Edith had made her life in Israel, had married, and had had

her children there. She came back to Belgium to attend the conference and to visit the family who had sheltered her. Among seven hundred participants, we saw one another by utter coincidence. For, notwithstanding the attendance's list, if we had not sat next to each other, we probably would not have met. We exchanged addresses and promised to stay in touch. In the confusion that followed the afternoon session, we neglected to make plans to meet again during the conference, I assumed that we would do so at some point anyway, now that we could spot one another by sight. However, I was disconcerted when, in searching for her on the second and last day of the gathering, I didn't find her.

Your classmate Louise from the convent school may have been there too.

Indeed, but we couldn't have met among the seven hundred people primarily because I couldn't remember her last name, neither could I remember the name of the school. People pinned messages on a bulletin board erected for the purpose of finding other people. I checked the board periodically, but Louise probably had forgotten my last name too. Therefore, neither of us could have looked for the other in the attendance list, and we didn't have enough information to pin on the bulletin board.

The day following the conference the organizers had arranged group visits to three sites: the concentration camp of Breendonk, the camp at the former Caserne Dossin in Malines where 25,257 Jews caught in Belgium were assembled for deportation to Auschwitz, and the Memorial in Anderlecht to the Jewish Martyrs and Jewish Resistance Fighters. This memorial bears on its walls the names of all the Jews deported from Belgium who perished. When, before the conference, I was informed of these visits and was requested to sign up if I wanted to participate, I was torn by anxiety and rejected the idea. It would all be too painful and to no avail, I thought. However, after long reflection I decided I was bound to go in reverence to my loved ones and all those who had died. Since they had no graves this visit corresponded to going to their grave site.

Three buses traveled from hotels and other meeting places. The participants in these visits were, in general, people who had come from overseas. The principal organizers of the conference, all residents and Belgian citizens, accompanied us. The first stop was Breendonk, a former fort dating back to the middle ages that was transformed into a concentration camp by the German SS.[36] It has been kept intact and is now a museum. We encountered there numerous groups of schoolchildren with their teachers. The prisoners who had been in this horrifying site were for the most part political, many of them resistance fighters. Although it was not set up as an extermination camp, the horror experienced by the inmates at the hands of their captors is clearly exposed and is devastating to the visitor. Breendonk was a torture camp where people were starved, worked to death, and executed. I had not known of any such concentration camp on Belgian soil. We walked through the camp, we saw it all: the barrack rooms, the cells, the torture chamber. Overcome with revulsion and sadness my husband and I finally went through the gates and left the dreadful grounds.

Returning to our bus to wait for our group, we met Edith Berger, who had just arrived on one of the other buses. She was on her way into the camp. I warned her of the experience. Notwithstanding the dismal place of encounter, we were delighted to find one another once more and chatted for a while. My husband snapped our picture, and I promised her a copy. As participants of the trip, we would meet again on the following two stops.

We were keenly aware of the contradiction between the drive on this sunny spring day through the charming Flemish countryside and villages, and our destination: Malines, a name associated with the dreaded camp where the trapped Jews were assembled for deportation. Malines, a town whose name still summons forth grief and shivers. The president of the Belgian organization *L'Enfant Caché de Belgique*, who rode on our bus, warned us at the start of this leg of our journey that the camp in the former Caserne Dossin, in the heart of the town, has been transformed and contains now *des apartments villas*, that is, dwellings similar to what in North America are called condominiums. We would be allowed to enter but must remain near the double doors at the edge of the courtyard in order not to disturb the occupants. If at first we were conscious of the absurdity between the sunny drive through the countryside and our objective, the incongruity of the transformed antechamber of death, into cheerful and charming housing was even more preposterous. The dreadful site that our loved ones experienced was now resplendent. Greeneries and flowers adorned balconies and the courtyard. As we crowded in the doorway to look, we tried to imagine it as it was before, dreadful and packed with our unfortunate martyrs. One survivor explained the procedure employed by the captors. He pointed to a room left untransformed, near the entrance. There the Nazis processed their victims upon their arrival. Now the town of Malines has donated that room to become a museum in memory of

At the left is Edith (Berger) Lavy, with the author. Breendonk, Belgium, May 1995.

the persecuted Jews deported from Belgium. The latter news consoled us somewhat, and we could hear workmen already busy at the task. Still, we remained shaken by the transformation.

Soon our organizers requested that we depart, fearful of disturbing the residents by the numbers in our group. We paused outside the building, facing the exterior wall of what was to become the museum, and examined the two tablets, one inscribed in Flemish and the other in French, counseling passersby to remember the many thousands of Jews who had been deported from 1942 to 1944 from that site. The railroad tracks for the cattle cars that sent the victims to their fate had come right up to the entrance of the caserne. The Belgian Jewish Community salvaged some tracks and placed six pieces of unequal lengths erect in front of the bilingual tablets to commemorate the victims. We placed collectively a sheaf of flowers on the tracks. Following a minute of silence, we said the Kaddish prayer.[37]

Seated again, we proceeded on our ride to Anderlecht, and the Anderlecht Memorial there. Some of us voiced our embitterment and shock that the Caserne Dossin, Maline's grievous historical landmark, had been transformed into luxury apartments. The president of the Belgian Jewish organization disagreed. She emphasized the Jewish Community's gratitude to the town of Malines for the donation of the one room for the purpose of the museum.[38]

The Memorial to the Jewish Martyrs and Freedom Fighters of Belgium in the municipality of Anderlecht rises in the former heart of the largest Jewish Community of greater Brussels. The gates are always locked, and access to the memorial must be arranged in advance. Inside the large cement enclosure three extensive walls display in alphabetical order the 25,257 names of the deported Jews from Belgium who perished at the hands of the German Nazis. As I entered I again encountered Edith, who had already found her father's name. I proceeded to scrutinize the walls. Again, it was a shock to find them; my sister Herta Krygier, her husband

The memorial tablets on the outside wall of the former
Caserne Dossin. Malines Belgium, May 1995.

Israel Krygier, my aunt Pepi Dermer, my two cousins Fred Dermer and Max Glasz. I stood staring at their names, touching the writing. They were all there, and I confronted once more the confirmation of their deaths. My sister was listed by her married name, so that for the first time I saw her husband's name inscribed next to hers. To see their names side by side was somehow comforting. She had been caught and deported when she went to search for his whereabouts. They were now together, inscribed on this wall, united forever in this monument.

A former Jewish Resistance fighter, decorated with numerous medals, led us to a separate enclave displaying the names of the Jews who had died fighting in the Belgian Resistance. Now, elderly and still bearing the signs of the wounds sustained, he elucidated his and some of the other Jewish fighters' bravery and daring in the Resistance, and answered questions. Continuously overcome with sadness, we all returned to the center of the larger memorial. We gathered around a small platform to recite again the Kaddish prayer. A tape recorder intoned Israel's national anthem *Hatikvah*, the symbol of Jewish rebirth, followed by the national anthem of Belgium, the *Brabançonne*. We joined in with fervor, thereby experiencing much-needed emotional release. Ever since those dark days of our childhood, before *Hatikvah*, meaning "hope" in Hebrew, became the national anthem of the State of Israel, its words and music conveyed to us our identity. With the *Brabançonne* we acknowledged the bond with the host country of the conference and our connection with Belgium through our past, as well as our feelings of appreciation to the Belgian people. Our singing affirmed us as Jews and survivors dedicated to transmitting the memory of our martyrs to future generations.

Milling around outside the boundaries of the memorial, I scanned the surroundings, which grew progressively more familiar. I immediately recognized, standing diagonally across from the memorial, the still functioning elementary school I had attended. Even *parc Rix*, the small park were I had played so often remains a block away. On the street signs I recognized names I had not said or heard spoken in half a century. Those names brought back images of school days before the persecution of Jews. This was the street that I took to school, and I walked on that other street when I stopped at a friend's before going home. For a moment the experience brought back the sweet feeling of childhood, the sad memories not withstanding.

We returned to our buses for the ride back to our hotels, dizzy and perturbed by the sum of the day's occurrences. Seated behind my husband and me were two women who were speaking German, a sound that I found very disturbing at that point. I knew that both spoke French and English, so I turned to them and requested that they speak either one of those languages. They apologized, explaining that they had known each other since early childhood and that German was the language they spoke with their parents. Of course I understood, since I too had spoken German with my parents. I excused myself in turn, but they appreciated my discomfort and continued their conversation in English.

Back at the hotel we said good-bye, and congratulated and thanked the organizers for all their efforts. I knew that I needed time to process all the emotions brought forth by the day's events. I also expected that the following days would require further emotional endurance in my search for the documentation for this book. I would have to cope with my nervousness and feelings of insecurity provoked by the prospect of this quest. We made arrangements to transfer our belongings to another hotel, where my husband and I would spend the following eleven days before returning to the United States.

Tracking down the Catholic boarding school and the day school that I had attended was the first objective on our itinerary the following day. Perhaps it no longer existed. All along its name had kept eluding me; however, I remembered its location and was fairly confident that I could find it. I apologized, to my husband, for my noticeable agitation and decided to do no driving, considering my state of mind. He assured me that he would handle it all; not to worry, he would get us there. In our small rented car we started out from the municipality of Ixelles, clear across town to the very limit of Anderlecht, with the thought of finding first the street and house where we lived in hiding during those dark years. I supposed that once we found the street, I would remember my way from there.

Although the surroundings of my first elementary school near the Jewish memorial remained familiar, the area that once was a rural district had changed completely. Wide roads and highways replaced streets where houses had stood in small, separate clusters. After asking for directions, we finally found *rue Adolphe Willemans*, now totally filled with houses, except for the field that still lies across from no. 197. The way I had walked to school was now blocked by a large shopping mall. Following some inquiries there, I found that indeed, the Catholic day school and boarding school still functioned. To get there was a bit complicated, but after crossing a main highway, I recognized in the distance the

The entrance to the National Memorial of the Jewish Martyrs of Belgium. Anderlecht, Brussels, May 1995.

steeple of the church. The hill where it stood, once over-spread with fields and trees, was now covered with houses. I learned what I had never realized so many years ago: my walk to school had led me into a different municipality, from Anderlecht to Dilbeek. A totally different environment surrounded the day and boarding schools. It was now a middle-class suburb. A densely populated neighborhood had replaced the agrarian scenery. Outside the day school, parents in cars waited for their children. And there, above the entrance, was the school's name: *Regina Ceali* (Queen of Heaven). Yes, of course, I had never paid much attention to the name in Latin. That was why it had vanished from my memory. Gradually the faint recollection emerged. Scanning the surroundings for recognizable landmarks, I noticed that buildings filled the site of the boarding school's earlier roller-skating rink. In search of familiar traces, we entered the boarding school grounds. Several students were having refreshments, sitting on a bench outside one of the buildings. I inquired as to the name of the order of the sisters who ran their school. They giggled, surprised by my question as well as by my addressing them in French. They answered, translating into French literally from the Flemish: *De Susters van Lievsde van Jesus en Maria van Gent.* (The Sisters of Love of Jesus and Mary of Gent). I discovered subsequently that the proper translation of the order's name was *The Sisters of Charity of Jesus and Mary of Gent.* Looking for an administrative office, my husband pointed out a notice displayed on a wall of the corridor, declaring that the reader was now in Flanders where Flemish is spoken, thus would he not also speak Flemish as well. After reading this notice we decided that we had better not wander about any longer, that instead we would begin our inquiry at the elementary school.

We proceeded through the gate of the day school, leading into the school yard filled with girls and boys at play during recess. The former all-girl school now had a mixed student body. Also, there were no sisters in sight. I recognized parts of the school yard and the covered entrance leading to the classrooms. Yes, I mused, this was where the teacher took our class on Good Friday afternoon; kneeling there, we had memorialized the death of Christ. As we attempted to enter the building with the thought of finding the principal, we were stopped by a voice coming from behind us. A teacher on duty during recess queried us rather sharply as to our motives. When I explained in French our wish to see the principal, she reminded us that this was a Flemish school. Furthermore, she continued visibly vexed, the principal was not in, and, she asked, did we have an appointment? For a minute I thought of my first elementary school located near the Anderlecht Memorial that I had seen the day before, and of the streets in its vicinity. I recalled the surprising feelings of pleasing impressions and emotions associated with the existence of childhood that the experience had brought forth. But the present encounter brought back only the sensations of insecurity experienced in this school so many years before. The verbal exchange with the teacher aroused memories of anxieties and alienation. I hastened to describe to her the reasons for our visit, explaining further that at the present time, her French was so superior to my Flemish that for the sake of expediency, it would be preferable for us to converse in the former. Her expression, upon hearing my story about having been one of two Jewish girls who clandestinely attended this school during the war, attested her surprise. No doubt she was taken aback. I asked whether the school was still run by the sisters. By now somewhat mollified, she replied that the faculty consisted of lay teachers, although it was still a Catholic school. She added that she had been teaching there for the past thirty years. I indicated that I wished to find someone who could consult the school's records in the hope of finding the last name of the other Jewish child, whereupon she pointed at the main administration building of the boarding school. "Go and ring the bell over there," she said. "That is the place where such information might be available." We followed her advice.

The door opened by means of an automatic device oper-

The memorial of the Jewish Resistance Fighters of
Belgium. Anderlecht, Brussels, May 1995.

ated from within. We found a friendly and very young woman who was the receptionist-telephone operator; replying in French, she advised us to speak to Mme Vandevelde, the head administrator, who unfortunately had just left. Therefore, we should telephone at a certain time the following morning.

I came away somewhat encouraged. I would speak the next day to someone in authority who might provide information and eventually help in consulting the school's old records. In addition, I had partly accomplished my quest by locating the school and unearthing its name that had lain buried in my memory.

We proceeded on our journey in search of further aspects of my childhood and set out for the former Jewish quarter to which I had never returned. I was uneasy at the notion of seeing the area and the house where, hiding in the cellar's closets, we had eluded the Nazis during their night raid of the neighborhood. I found the former lower-middle and working-class neighborhood extremely deteriorated. Dilapidated automobiles packed the earlier tree-and bench-lined middle strip of the *Boulevard de la Révision,* where I had played with Edith Berger, her siblings, and other friends. The house on the corner of *rue de l'Instruction* with its *brasserie* on the ground floor, where we had lived in the pitiable garret dwelling, was still there, now grimy and somewhat decayed. In my memory it had seemed fairly substantial, and the boulevard quite ample. It all appeared shrunken to the adult standing there, from the impressions of an eight-year-old. I pointed out the room on the second floor which we had occupied after descending from the garret, and its corner balcony where we had stood on Mother's Day 1940 after we had heard the unfamiliar sound of gunfire and looked up at an airplane dogfight. We turned the corner onto *rue de l'Instruction* and stopped at number 127. That house was in fairly good condition, and its size looked exactly as I remembered. I stared at the two cellar windows; they were the same ones that rose above the two small closets where we had hidden during the Nazi night raid. I asked my husband to take a picture but declined his suggestion to be in it. Looking about, I noticed that the street that led to my sister's former apartment was sealed off by a major transformation project. I decided to forgo finding that house on *rue de France*. The search would be very painful and for no purpose. I was eager to withdraw from the neighborhood altogether.

The following day, as planned, I phoned the *Regina Ceali Lyceum* and spoke to Mme Vandevelde. I apologized for speaking French, and our conversation was very cordial. From the tone of her remarks and the content of her questions, it was evident to me that the information I conveyed to her regarding the school's harboring of two Jewish children during the German occupation, was a revelation. I informed her of my writing regarding my childhood experiences. She replied with skepticism to my inquiries about consulting school records that would enable me to trace the name and whereabouts of my Jewish classmate Louise. First of all, she doubted that any of the people who staffed the school during those years were still alive, and she wondered whether records had been kept dating back to that period. I mentioned the fact that Louise had been baptized by the nuns. Therefore, didn't she think that this baptism would be registered? She promised to investigate and to phone me within the next two days. I didn't hear from her, and so I again took the initiative. Yes, she had made inquiries. Indeed, the personnel who had staffed the school in those years had passed on, and in addition, she had spoken to the present principal, who told her that no records dating back so far were on hand. As to the baptism, it had most likely been done in the school, and since the whole procedure was clandestine and dangerous for the nuns, she herself, as well as people whom she had consulted, doubted very much that anything had been noted in writing. In any case, nothing could be found presently. However, she would keep the matter in mind and would write to me in the United States should she discover anything further.

More than one year has elapsed since our last conversa-

The house on rue de l'Instruction. On the lower right is one of the basement windows under which we hid in tiny closets during the Germans' night raid, in 1942. Anderlecht, Brussels, May 1995.

tion. I have had no word from Mme Vandevelde and have come to the conclusion that no additional information will be forthcoming. I know that Louise eluded the Nazis because I had met her after the Liberation. Therefore, I have resolved to hope and assume that she is well and lives somewhere happily with family and friends.

The *Musée Juif de Belgique* (Jewish Museum of Belgium) was the next stop on my itinerary, and the sequence of events that followed was to be all positive. I am obliged and thankful to the *Musée* for making available to me much of the documentation needed for this writing. I had envisioned consuming an indefinite time searching government archives. However, with the assistance of the museum's curator, Mr. Daniel Dratwa, I found most of the documentation within two days. The hours spent researching in the museum library resulted in satisfying and useful discoveries as well as in encountering other people on similar quests. In addition, under the curator's guidance I located more information at the *Menorah Librairie Hébraïque*, a bookstore of Jewish interest and at the *Institut d'Etudes du Judaïsme, Institut Martin Buber* (Institute of Jewish Studies, Buber Institute), the latter on the university campus of the ULB *(Université Libre de Bruxelles.)*. The interest and assistance of the Institut's staff was most gratifying. Among other things, they tracked down books in Flemish that might possibly furnish additional documents. After numerous phone calls, they found them available at the bookstore of the VUB *(Vrije Universiteit Brussel)*, the Flemish equivalent of the French-language ULB, adjacent to the latter campus.

Inadvertently, I was also able to make contact with some people who had belonged to the Austrian youth movement that I had joined as a very young teenager after the Liberation. I had questioned the *Musée's* curator as to whether he had any information concerning this organization, since I wanted to describe its purpose and its location at that time. He had no information himself, but he gave me the name and phone number of a man who he said was knowledgeable about Jewish-Austrian affairs in Belgium. Somehow that name stayed in my mind; it seemed familiar, and I kept thinking about it all the next day. I had an inkling that I knew this person. Finally, I had a strong notion of who he was. When I phoned him, my expectation proved to be correct. Indeed, he said, he had been a member and for a time the senior advisor to the youth group. When I inquired why he had not participated in the *Hidden Children's* conference that had just ended, he explained that he had not been a hidden child and thus did not belong there. He could not recognize who I was at that moment, but he invited me and my husband for coffee on Saturday afternoon. We would then be able to get reacquainted. He mentioned the names of two sisters, former hidden children whom I remembered from the group. He had just seen them, but unfortunately they had already left. They had come from Switzerland and Germany to attend the conference. The meeting proved to be very enjoyable. We saw Karl, now Charles and his wife Mili, who had also been a member of the youth organization. They had invited their neighbors, Mili's brother Sigi and his wife Susi, both of whom had also met in the group, also Heinz, now Henri, and his wife whom I had not known before. They had all remained living in Brussels. When we were in the youth organization they were considered the older members. I recognized Karl and Sigi immediately, and after a while Susi and Heinz as well. I would not have recognized Mili even though I had known her very well. I was surprised when they said that they recognized me at once. We discussed many topics connected with our families' situations before, during, and after the war. We spoke of the *Comité des Refugiés*, the internment camps, among others *Merxplas* where my father had spent several months and where Sigi, I found out that afternoon, had spent a whole year. I learned about the background of the former youth organization.[39] We discussed the younger members with whom I had belonged and considered the different needs that the group fulfilled for them. I remembered how painful had been that period in my adolescence. It was the time when we searched in vain for the names of our loved ones on lists of survivors, when my mother, as soon as she spotted an emaciated survivor would run to him or her with my sister's picture. On the other hand, it was also an era of optimism, of confidence in the years to come. The energy of youth surmounted all insecurity. We had survived, the future looked bright.

And so we met again almost fifty years later. Pictures were brought out as well as old song books. I remembered most of the songs and, with enthusiasm, we sang them again.

Thus, after many trying stops in the course of this journey to return to the places of my childhood, the quest ended on a positive note. I had had many misgivings and anxieties about participating in the conference. I reconnected with my past and learned much important and useful information from this gathering of former hidden children. I encountered friends whom I never expected to see again; and I met wonderful people who facilitated the writing of this book. I am glad then to have returned to Belgium on my quest.

THE BOX

I had to come to the end of my writing this book finally to summon the will and strength to overcome my weakness so that I could examine the papers in "the box."

I discovered some items that I had expected to find, but others that I had assumed would be there were missing. In addition, I uncovered some items that I didn't know existed. First of all, I found my sister's school certificates, starting with elementary school from 1927 to 1931, from age six to ten, and also her certificates from 1932 to 1935, of the *Öffentliche Hauptschule für Mädchen in Wien,* a secondary school; and finally I discovered two half year certificates of the 1931-32 school-year from the *Chajesrealgymnasium des Vereins "Jüdisches Real gymnasium" Wien.* These indicate something that I hadn't known, that she had attended simultaneously a state school and a Jewish school. All of the certificates carry the mention of *sehr gut* (very good), just as I had always been told by my family.

I found her postcards from Malines. However, I couldn't locate the letter that she wrote right before she was deported. Her comments to me recommending that I look after my parents, since she could no longer do so, remained with me always (see page 105). I also searched in vain for the postcard that she had written in code from Auschwitz (see pages xiii, 10-11, 135-136). This item stands out clearly in my memory, especially since we pondered so long over the meaning of its content. The missing letter and the missing postcard, might have been sent by my parents to their attorney when they tried to obtain a pension from the German Government. Their lawyer may have submitted the letter as proof of her devotion to her family, and the postcard as proof of her detention in that death camp. I phoned the law office and found that this attorney died some years ago after he retired, and no one knew the whereabouts of his clients' files. I was promised that inquiries would be made, but never heard anything further.

But I found several letters that she had thrown out of the train, as well as notes from the people who had found them and forwarded them. Her encouraging words to us for the future, and her hope and expectation of her husband's eventual arrival in Brussels from the north of France, are heartbreaking. The people sent to the north of France were put to work along the coast of the English Channel, where they labored like convicts under extreme conditions and with hardly any food. They were housed in three camps, Israel I, II, and III. Of the deported Jews 196 escaped, that is, 8 percent of the said manpower, mostly en route from the camp to the work site at a distance of about ten kilometers. Ultimately they were shipped to Malines, where at the end of 1942, 1,893 of them left for Auschwitz in the last convoys of that year.[40] We now know that only several days after her own deportation, Herta's husband was also on his way to Auschwitz from the north of France via Malines (see pages 169-170).

The writing on most of the letters and postcards has faded and is difficult to read. It can hopefully be enhanced and reproduced with the use of modern technology. Contrary to what I had thought, my sister hadn't sent the postcards and letters to our old address in Anderlecht, the place where we had eluded the Nazis in tiny closets during the night raid (pages. 99-101, 105). Rather, she sent them to a Mr. Müller at 51 rue Poiçon in Brussels, for reasons of security on our behalf. I have a vague recollection of this Mr. Müller's being one of my father's coworkers and not Jewish. Thus it was from this man that my father retrieved her letters (see page 135). Her letters consoling us and reassuring us are heart-rending. And pitiful are her hopes that her husband might send home his salary, that he might be returning, as are her recommendations for him, and her wish that we should kiss him for her, when unbeknown to us all, he was already on the way to the same fate as hers.

The most astounding discovery was a postcard from my brother-in-law Srulek, which again for security reasons was addressed to a good friend and neighbor, Mme Gabin (see pages 108-109). The postcard is written in German by someone else, but the card was signed "Krigier." Since Srulek's last name was spelled "Krygier," this signature is therefore misspelled. I cannot say whether or not this is actually my brother-in-law's signature, since I don't know his handwriting. The Gabins didn't know German, but it was a good means to get the postcard past the censors, who would be able to read it. The postcard bears the name of the *Association des Juifs de Belgique*, meaning that it was forwarded under the Association's auspices and bears no postmark. It gives Srulek's name with an address as: *Haus No.10, Fawischowitz, Arbeitslager* (work camp). The writer dates the postcard October 6, 1943. I was unaware of this communication. It shows that after being shipped from the north of France via Malines to Auschwitz on October 31, 1942, he was still alive nearly one year later. Sadly, he didn't survive until liberation.

At last, with the final task of examining the contents of "the box," I have fulfilled the mission that I had imposed upon myself. What has it meant to write this book? During the interval between the first gathering of former hidden children in New York City, and the journey back to the places of my childhood and the last conference in Brussels, I have come full circle. The process of recalling and recording the events of those years was often unbearable and had to be interrupted in order to regain energy and courage. The memory will always be hurtful, but through this process of writing, I have renewed my connections with my past and with my loved ones. I feel that I have brought them back into the light. I owe it to them to make their stories known, to pass this history on to my children and grandchildren who deserve to know it, for it is our history.

Chapter X

TRANSLATED
LETTERS AND POSTCARDS

The following postcard, badly faded and barely readable, was sent from Malines (Mechelen in Flemish) Sammellager Dossin (Assembly camp Dossin) 453 XIV, on October 20, 1942.

. . . . write readably. My neighbor lies in bed. Toothbrush, paste, washcloth, scrubbing brush, shoe cleaning kit all that you find of mine. My blanket / . . . spoon. What is in the red bag, leave it all, what won't go in send in a burlap sack. Bread . . . sanitary napkins in the cabinet, yes don't forget. There are many people here who have worked with Srulek. It's ok here. People have even bedding with them. Theater is being performed. Mama, Papa, Inge stay strong so that in health we can again be together. You should always. . . .

See pgs. 199 & 210

Note to the finder on the envelope:

"You are begged to help an unfortunate one and put this in the mail-box. You are thanked in advance."

See pgs. 200 & 210

October 24, 1942

My dear ones beloved:

Now it's starting, we are riding the time passes and I still believe it is only a dream. Well don't worry I am really ok, *there are eight of us in a compartment, the shoemaker's wife and her son are here too, all of us . . . entertain fine. With food we are well supplied, bread, a steamed shnitzel, indeed to be seen with opera glasses, apple, tomatoes and honey, we are getting a sweet trip; besides the kitchen rides along so there is soup and "Eintopfgericht."* Besides you have supplied me well. I thank you a 1000 times for everything but now look after yourselves you must stay healthy and strong careful my dearest and always stay together. Don't let Inge go by herself any longer. I have already thrown out two letters and a card for you and a letter for the manager and Gabin. Yesterday I received a fifth parcel and a fifth letter from you and I was very happy but now I am glad that you can no longer send me anything otherwise you would soon be broke. No, don't be angry, of course my parents take their shirt off for me, long life to you, ** but I absolutely don't agree. You can be at ease yesterday I received beside your dear package also two packages from Ezra*** one with food and one with warm underwear. 3 undershirts and 3 underpants and a scarf with cap everything prime warm, wool. So, no worries, I am well supplied. Write to my Srulek and kiss him for me when he comes, he should hide well and eat. My dear ones don't save on food; Gabin will give you 250 francs for my coal, when the women from Meune comes, the manager should take the money 650 francs pay for the gas and electricity and take a kilo tobacco for Papa and give you the rest. If money comes from Srulek, the manager should take it and give it to you. If you need money, take it above the table one meter from the window. Sell what you want. So my dear ones,the train shakes and us with it, surely we ride very elegantly 3rd. class passenger car, complaining would be sinful for we already rode half an hour in a cattle car, well that was something. Personally I don't mind, but small children and old people that is very hard. So don't worry I am young and you are too. Please don't cry and now always think of yourselves until in a few weeks or even sooner I am again with you. I'll also bring Aunt and Fredi along, just you stay there. Be very careful, never go to my apartment. So be kissed 10000 times each one sepa-*

rately from all my heart and till we meet soon and happily again. Your loving Herta. Kiss me my Srulek. In case God forbid Srulek comes to Malines, he should ask for my number.

* All ingredients cooked together.

** That is, I love you.

*** Jewish service organization.

See pgs 201-202 & 210-211

October 24

My dear ones!

We have been sitting several hours in the train and are approximately near Liège (Lüttich). I hasten to write to you a few words as long as we are still in Belgium. Our train goes very slowly. We will probably ride 4 days. There are almost 20 cars full of people. Almost 1800. Many small children and old people. We the young ones hope that over there we'll be separated from them; such people are really a torment. In our compartment we are young women and the boy from the shoemaker's wife from rue de l'Instruction 123. She sends you her heartfelt greetings. For now, we are still ok. One sleeps, another eats, the others chatter, always merry, that is the best way to get through in the world. So, no worries, you do have confidence in me and I hope and believe I won't disappoint you. We were told that the weather over there is good. I am convinced that for us too the sun will soon shine again. We halted again. We have a real snail's pace. The people are taking the letters and give us signs that they understand us. I hope and pray to God that you receive my letters. I write as long as I still have paper. As much as I tried and wanted to it was impossible for me to find out anything at the Caserne. My money, watch and identification card all are gone, in return we each received a dog number. So my dear ones do not worry, God is with me and should protect all of you. Stay in good health there and be real careful. Be kissed a 1000 times from all my heart in loving Your Herta.

Herta put the preceding letter in a makeshift envelope with the following words to the finder:

"You are begged to put this in the letter-box , help an unfortunate one. Thank you very much.."

The finder added this note:

"They have gone <u>east</u>."

See pgs 203-204 & 212

Postcard, 25/Oct./42

My Dearest Ones!

We are sitting in the train and the trip to the unknown has begun. We are all in good spirits. Eight of us sit in a compartment. The shoemaker's wife and her boy are here too. We are all on first name basis and address each other using "Du" [informal]. So far I have thrown out for you 3 letters and a card. I think one letter fell under the train. I have also written one letter to the manager and to Gabin. I'll write to them another card and then its finished. I thank you 1000 times for what you have sent me, I am really ok with food and drink We are supplied and you have really supplied me. . . I am very happy that you also have understood regarding the apartment, a stone fell from my heart. I always think of all of you. Stay healthy. So my dearest ones stay strong and well and until our early and happy reunion. Hello to everyone kiss my Srulek 10000 kisses for everyone separately, your loving Herta.

See pgs 205-213

Herta threw out of the train the following note addressing the finder:

Esteemed Finder. I call on your good heart to do a kind and Godly deed. Help unfortunate parents receive news from their children, you yourself may have children in the field and will understand what it means to receive a few words from them. Please put the letter enclosed in this cover with the address on the back in a regular envelope. Thousand Thanks .

She enclosed the following letter:

Oct.26.42

My dear ones!

Am sending you heartfelt greetings from our trip through beautiful Germany. We passed Kassel and Hall on the Saale yesterday. We are really making a nice journey. The weather here is very nice. I feel well. So, stay well. Heartfelt kisses to all of you your loving Herta.

The finder sent the preceding communications with the following message:

27.Oct.42 I am sending you the enclosed letter which I found on the railroad section of Schnellenwalde O/S (Ober Schlesien). Hopefully I have thereby really brought you happiness. Although I have no children in the field, nevertheless I can understand what great joy it must be to receive once more news from children and missing wives. And so then I have taken Miss Herta's letter in the desired form to the post office in the hope that you will also receive it well. Although we don't know each other, receive good greetings from

Ed. Herrmann. <u>*Heil Hitler.*</u>

See Pgs 206-208, 213, 214

The following is a postcard from Srulek addressed to Mme

Gabin, sent via the *Association des Juifs de Belgique* from "Haus No. 10 Workcamp Fawischowitz O/Sch (Ober Schlesien). October 6, 1943:

Dear Mrs. Gabin:

I am letting you know that I am here and well. I work and am satisfied. I hope that you are well and that you'll answer me soon. Many heartfelt greetings from

your

Krigier

See pgs 209 & 214

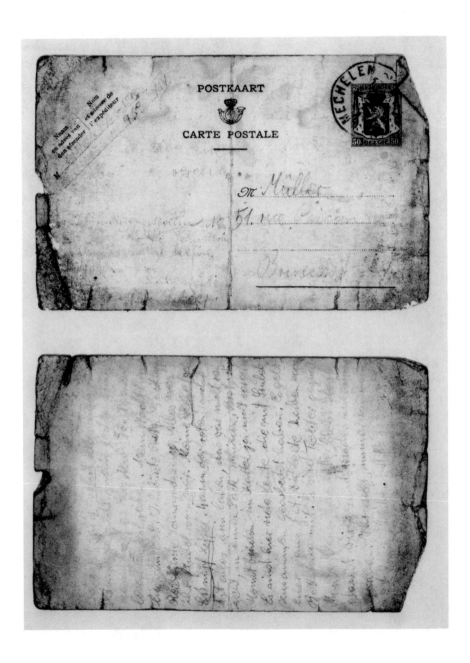

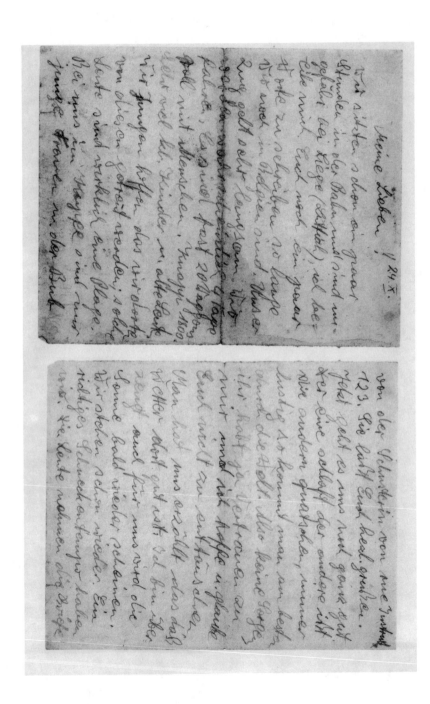

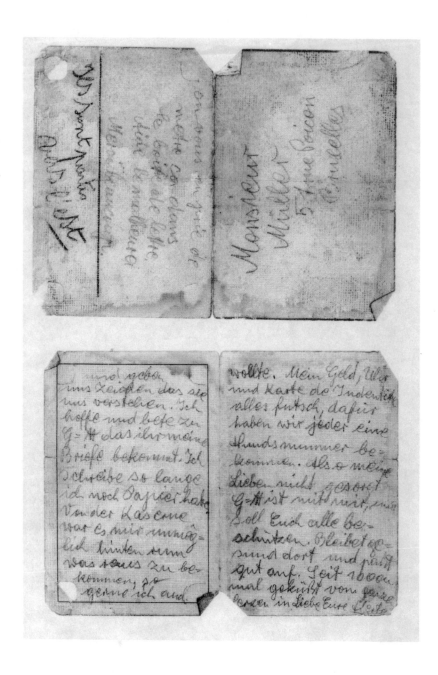

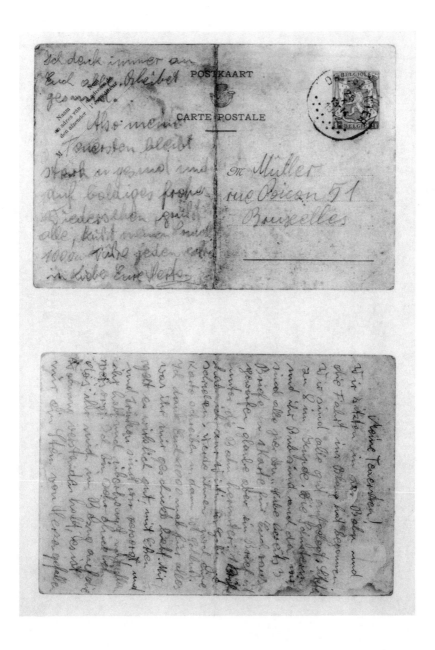

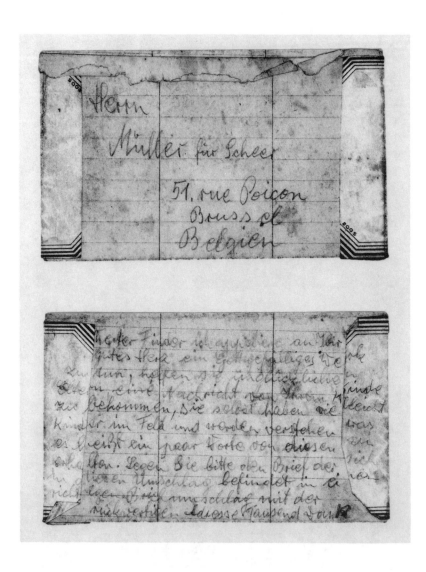

26. X. 42.

Meine Lieben!
Sende Euch die herzlichsten
Grüße von meiner Reise
durchs schöne Deutsch-
land. Wir passierten
gestern Kassel und
Halle a.d. Saale. Wir machen
wirklich eine schöne Reise.
Das Wetter hier ist sehr
schön. Ich fühle mich sehr
gut; Also bleibet gesund.
Es küßt Euch alle herzlich in Liebe
Eure ...

27.10.42

Anbei sende ich Ihnen beiliegenden
Brief, den ich auf der Bahnstrecke
gefunden hatte bei Schmellwalde(?)...
Hoffentlich habe ich Ihnen wirklich
eine Freude damit gemacht. Ich habe
zwar keine Kinder im Felde stehen,
kann aber trotzdem verstehen, wenn
man wieder mal Nachricht von
den Kindern auch weiter hören

erhält, wie groß dann die Freude
ist. Und so habe ich denn den Brief
von Frl. Herta in der gewünschten
Form zur Post gegeben in der
Hoffnung, daß Sie ihn auch gut
erhalten.
Nun seien Sie auch bestens
gegrüßt unbekannter Weise
von Fr. Herrmann. Heil Hitler!

ASSOCIATION DES JUIFS EN BELGIQUE
Fondée en vertu de l'ordonnance
de l'Autorité Occupante du 2 / 1 / 1942
COMITE DIRECTEUR
SERVICE D'INTERVENTIONS

Nouvelle adresse :
Bd d'Anvers, 36
Nieuw adres :
Antwerpschelaan, 36

Absender: *Israel Kruger*
Straße: *Haus N. 10*
Ort: *Zawischowitz*
Arbeitslager

Postkarte

Herrn
Gabin
Brüssel

Straße, Hausnummer, Gebäudeteil, Stockwerk

Zawischowitz d. 10.6.43

Liebe Frau Gabin!
Ich teile Ihnen mit, daß ich hier mich
gesund befinde. Ich arbeite u. bin zu-
frieden. Ich hoffe, daß es auch Euch gut
geht u. Sie mir bald antworten.
Viele herzl. Grüße von
Ihrem
Kruger

The following letters and postcards are transcribed as closely as possible from the originals, including, with a few exceptions, the original punctuation and spelling.

Sammellager Dossin 453 XIV Postkaart 20.Oct.42

. . . . leselich schreiben. Meine Nachtbarin liegt im Bett. Zahnbürste, Paster, Waschlappen, Reibbürste, Schuhpuzzeug alles was ihr finded von mir. Meine Decke /. . . Essnapf Löffel. Was in der roten Tasche ist alles drin lassen, das was nicht rein geht in einem Sack schicken. Brot . . . Monatsbinden im Kastel ja nicht vergessen. Es sind hier viele Leute die mit Srulek zusammen gearbeitet haben. Es geht hier ganz gut. Die Leute haben sogar Bettzeug mit. Es wird Theater gespielt. Mama, Papa, Inge bleibt stark damit wir gesund wieder zusammen kommen. Ihr solt immer. . . .

Note to the finder on the envelope:

"On vous en prie d'aider une malheureuse et de mettre ça dans la boite à lettre. On vous remercie d'avance".

24/X

Meine lieben Teueren.

Nun geht es los, wir fahren schon die Zeit fergeht und ich glaube immer es ist blos ein Traum. Also keine Sorge es geht mir wirklich gut, wir sind hier zu 8 im Kupee, die Schusterin und ihr Bub sind auch da, wir sind alle . . . . unterhalten fein. Mit Essen sind wir gut versorgt, ein Brot, ein verdünstes Schnitzel, allerdings mit den Opernglass zu beschauen, Apfel, Tomaten, Honig, man macht uns eine süsse Reise; ausserdem fährt die Küche mit also gibt es Suppe und Eintopfgericht. Ausserdem habt Ihr mich auch sehr gut versorgt. Ich danke Euch 1000 mal für alles aber jetzt schaut auf Euch ihr müsst gesund und stark bleiben. Lasst Inge ja nicht mehr allein gehen. Habe bereits zwei Briefe und 1 Karte für Euch und einen Brief für die Wirtin und Gabin heraus geworfen. Habe gestern ein 5 Paket und 5 Brief von Euch erhalten und mich sehr gefreut, aber jezt bin ich froh das ihr mir nichts mehr schicken könnt, sonst wäret ihr bald stier. Nein, seit nicht bös, natürlich meine Eltern ziehen das Hemd für mich aus (ihr sollt mir leben), aber ich bin absolut nicht einverstanden. Ihr könnt beruhigt sein habe gestern ausser Euren lieben Paket noch 2 Pakete erhalten von der Esra bekommen eines mit Essen und 1 mit warmer Wäsche. 3 Hemden u. 3 Hosen 1 Schaal mit Kappe alles prima warm, Wolle. Also keine Sorgen, bin gut versorgt. Schreibt meinen Srulek und küsst ihm von mir wenn er kommt, er soll sich verstecken und essen. Meine Lieben spart nicht am Essen; Gabin wird Euch 250 Fr. für meine Kohlen geben, wenn die Goite von Meune kommt, die Wirtin soll das Geld nehmen 650 Fr. Gas & Elek. bezahlen & ein Kilo Tabak für Papa nehmen den Rest Euch geben. Wenn Geld von Srulek kommt, die Wirtin soll es nehmen und Euch geben. Falls Ihr Geld braucht nehmt Euch obern Tisch ein Meter von Fenster. Verkauft was ihr wollt. Also meine Lieben die Bahn wakelt und wir mit, wir fahren doch sehr elegant 3 Klasse Personenwagen, nur nicht gesündigt, wir sind auch schon eine l/2 Stunde Viehwagen gefahren, no das war allerhand. Mir persönlich macht das nichts, aber kleine Kinder und alte Leute das ist schon sehr schwer. Also nicht gesorgt ich bin jung und ihr auch. Ja nicht weinen und jetzt nur noch an Euch denken bis ich in einiger Wochen oder noch früher wieder bei Euch bin. Ich bring auch Tante und Fredi mit, bleibt Ihr nur dort. Sehr aufpassen, geht nie wieder in meine Wohnung. Also seit 10000 mal geküsst, jeder extra von ganzen Herzen und baldiges frohes Wiedersehen. Eure Euch liebende Herta. Küsst mir meinen Srulek. Falls Srulek Gott behüte nach Maline kommt soll er sich nach meiner Nummer fragen.

24.X.

Meine Lieben !

*Wir sitzen schon ein paar Stunden in der Bahn und sind
ungefär bei Liege (Lüttich), Ich beeile mich Euch noch ein paar
Worte zy schreiben so lange wir noch in Belgien sind. Unser
Zug geht sehr langsam. Wir werden warscheindlich 4 Tage
fahren. Es sind fast 20 Wagone voll mit Menschen. Knappe
1800. Sehr viel kleine Kinder und alte Leute. Wir jungen
hoffen dass wir dorten von diesen getrennt werden; solche Leute
sind wirklich eine Plage. Bei uns im Koupee sind wir junge
Frauen und der Bub von der Schusterin von rue Instruction 123.
Sie Lässt Euch herzlich grüssen. Jetzt geht es uns noch ganz
gut. Der eine schläft, der andere isst, die anderen quatschen,
immer lustig so kommt man im Leben durch die Welt. Also
keine Sorgen, Ihr habt ja Vertrauen zu mir und ich hoffe und
glaube Euch nicht zu entäuschen. Man hat uns erzählt dass
das Wetter dort gut ist. Ich bin überzeugt auch für uns wird die
Sonne bald wieder Scheinen. Wir stehen schon wieder. Ein
richtiges Schneckentempo haben wir. Die Leute nehmen die
Briefe und geben Zeichen das sie uns verstehen. Ich hoffe und
bete zu Gott dass Ihr meine Briefe bekommt. Ich schreibe so
lange ich noch Papier habe. Von der Kaserne war es mir
unmöglich hinten rum was raus zu bekommen, so gerne ich
auch wollte. Mein Geld, Uhr und Karte d'Identite alles futsch,
dafür haben wir eine Hundenummer bekommen. Also meine
Lieben nicht gesorgt, Gott ist mit uns und soll Euch alle
beschützen. Bleibt gesund dort und passt gut auf. Seit 1000
mal geküsst von ganzen Herzen in Liebe Eure Herta.*

Herta put the preceding letter in a makeshift envelope with
the following words to the finder:

*"On vous en prie de mettre ça dans la boite à lettre. Aidez la
malheureuse. Merci beaucoup'.*

The finder added the following words:

Ils sont partis vers l'<u>est</u>.

Postkaart postmarked 25/Oct./42

Meine Teuersten !

Wir sitzen in der Bahn und die Fahrt ins Blaue hat begonnen. Wir sind alle gut aufgelegt. Sitzen zu 8 im Koupee. Die Schusterin und ihr Bub sind auch da, wir sind alle per Du. Habe bereits 3 Briefe und eine Karte für Euch rausgeworfen, glaube dass ein Brief ist unter die Bahn herunter. 1 Brief hab ich an die Wirtin une Gabin geschrieben. Werde ihnen noch eine Karte schreiben und dann ist schluss. Ich danke Euch 1000 mal für alles was Ihr mir geschickt habt. Mir geht es wircklich gut, mit Essen und Trinken sind wir versorgt, und Ihr habt mich überhaubt . . . . . versorgt. Ich bin sehr glücklich dass Ihr mich Bezug auf die Wonung verstanden habt, es ist mir ein Stein vom Herzen gefallen. Ich denke immer an Euch alle. Bleibt gesund. Also meine Teuersten bleibt stark und gesund und auf baldiges Wiedersehen. Grüsst alle, küsst meinen Srulek 10000 Küsse jeden einzeln, in Liebe Eure Herta.

Herta threw out of the train the following note addressing the finder:

Werter Finder. Ich appeliere an Ihr gutes Herz ein Gottgefälliges Werk zu tun, helfen Sie unglücklichen Eltern eine Nachricht von Ihren Kindern zu bekommen, Sie selbst haben vielleicht Kinder im Feld und werden verstehen was es heisst ein paar Worte von diesen zu erhalten. Legen Sie bitte den Brief das sich in diesen Umschlag befindet in einen richtigen Briefumschlag mit der rückwertige Adresse. Tausend Dank.

She enclosed the following letter:

26.X.42

Meine Lieben!

Sende Euch die herzlichsten Grüsse von meiner Reise durchs schöne Deutschland. Wir passierten Gestern Kassel und Hall a.d. Saale. Wir machen wirklich eine schöne Reise. Das Wetter ist sehr schön. Ich füle mich sehr gut. Also bleibt gesund. Es küsst Euch alle herz. in Liebe

Eure Herta

The finder sent the preceding communication with the following message:

27.10.42 Anbei sende ich Ihnen beiligenden Brief den ich auf der Bahnstrecke gefunden hatte bei Schnellenwalde o/S. Hoffentlich habe ich Ihnen wirklich eine Freude damit gemacht. Ich habe zwar keine Kinder im Felde stehn, kann aber trozdem verstehen wenn man wieder mal Nachricht von Kindern und vermisten Frauen erhält, wie gross dann die Freude ist. Und so habe ich dann den Brief von Fräulein Herta in der gewünschten Form zur Post gegeben in der Hoffnung dass Sie ihn auch gut erhalten.

Nun seien Sie auch bestens gegrüsst unbekanter Weise

von Ed. Herrmann. <u>*Heil Hitler*</u>

!

The following is a postcard from Srulek addressed to Mme Gabin, sent via the *Association des Juifs de Belgique* from:

"Haus No. 10 Fawischowitz o/Sch. Arbeitslager."

Fawischowitz d. 10.6.43

Liebe Frau Gabin !

Ich teile Ihnen mit, dass ich mich hier gesund befinde. Ich arbeite u. bin zufrieden. Ich hoffe, dass es Euch auch gut geht u. Sie mir bald antworten.

Viele herz. Grüsse von

Ihrem

Krigier

NOTES & REFERENCES

1. As of May 27, 1991, the organization was named The Hidden Child Foundation / ADL, with headquarters in New York City.

2. Klarsfeld, Serge, co-auther with Steinberg, Maxime, of *Mémorial de la Déportation des Juifs de Belgique*, listing the 25,257 Jews deported from Belgium who perished in Nazi death camps.

3. The Dossin barracks in Malines "were occupied by the Nazis and used for a criminal purpose, that is, as a collection point and holding pen for the Jews prior to deporting them to death camps." Pro Museo Judaico V.Z.W., p. 2. *The Malines Museum of Deportation and Resistance*, Michel Laub, C.C.I.B., Brussels, June 1995.

4. Elon, Amos, *Report from Vienna*, New Yorker, May 1991. Miller, Judith, *One, by One, by One*, pages 61-62. Simon and Schuster, New York, 1990.

5. See Maxime Steinberg, 1942 *Les Cents Jours de la Déportation des Juifs de Belgique*. Vie Ouvrière, Bruxelles, Belgique, 1984. Mr. Steinberg relates in detail how, within three months 17,000 Jews were tricked and rounded up by the Nazis for deportation to death camps.

6. *Shivah.* "Hebrew meaning 'seven'; the name given to the seven days of mourning for the dead." "This period of

grief . . . is incumbent upon the closest of kin only for the loss of father or mother, wife or husband, son or daughter, brother or sister." Nathan Ausubel, *The Book of Jewish Knowledge*, p. 403. Crown Publishers, Inc., New York, 1964.

7. "In 1938 Austrian Jews were permitted to take only thirty marks (later reduced to only ten) in German and foreign currency when they left Austria." Pauley, Bruce F., "Austria," in David Wyman and Charles H. Rosenzweig, *The World Reacts to the Holocaust*, pgs. 490-491. The Johns Hopkins University Press, Baltimore and London, 1996.

8. See Steiger, Sebastian, *Die Kinder von Schloss La Hille*, Volumes I and II, Brunnen-Verlag, Basel, 1992.

9. *Le Comité d'Assistance aux Réfugiés Juifs* provided financial assistance in 1939 to 7,351 persons who fled from the Greater Reich, i.e., Germany and Austria. Steinberg, Maxime, *La Question Juive, 1940-1942*, p. 82, Vie Ouvrière, Bruxellles, 1983. At the onset of the refugees' arrival, the funds were supplied by the local Jewish Community. As the problem grew, funds were contributed by the Jewish organizations of Great Britain and the U.S. However, the bulk of the funds came from the American Jewish Joint Distribution Committee. Caestecker, Frank, *Ongewenste Gasten*, p. 282. VUBPRESS, Brussels, 1993.

10. *Musee Juif de Belgique, Bruxelles*. Exposition: du 2 avril au 16 septembre 1995, Catalogue par Zahava Seewald sous la direction de Daniel Dratwa. Traces de la Mémoire: 1945-1995. "H. C. AFFICHE 'BABY POLA' Ed. A. S. Maccabi - imp. Impribelge Bruxelles - 1948. Texte français 73 x 54 cm (Don B. Guzu-Polak) Soirée artistique par l'association sportive Maccabi au Palais des Beaux-Arts de Bruxelles le 18 janvier 1948. La chanteuse Bertha Polak d'origine viennoise surnommée Baby Pola arrive à Bruxelles en 1938."

11. For another view of Merxplas from one detainee's experience there, see Fabry, Joseph, *The Next-to-Final Solution, A Belgian Detention Camp for Hitler Refugees*. Peter Lang Pub-

lishing Inc., New York, 1991. And for a totally different point of view of Merxplas, see Garfinkels, Betty, *Belgique, terre d'accueil: Problèmes du Refugié 1933-1940.* Editions Labor, Bruxelles, 1974.

12. Farby, Joseph, ibid. Mr. Farby states that he, as well as some of his fellow internees, were free to leave Merxplas only after obtaining a visa to another country, enabling them to leave Belgium.

13. As of May 10, 1940, the Belgian authorities arrested all men considered "suspect," targeting people of the extreme right as well as of the extreme left. Among those arrested were foreigners from enemy countries. Paradoxically, no exceptions were made for the German and Austrian Jews, victims of Nazi persecution who had come to Belgium seeking refuge. It did not matter whether or not they had answered the call of Jewish organizations and volunteered, as did 4,431 of them, when in 1939 the Belgian government called for mobilization. They were interned in the infamous camps in the south of France, such as Gurs and Riversaltes, among others. Steinberg, Maxime, *La Question Juive 1940-1942*, pgs. 85-87.

14. Line of fortification along the eastern frontier of France, extending from the Swiss border to the Belgian border. Named after André Maginot (1877-1932), French politician and war minister from 1929-1932. *Nouveau Petit Dictionnaire Larousse*, p. 1502. Librairie Larousse, Paris, 1971.

15. See Steinberg, Maxime, *La Question Juive 1940-1942*, p. 87. Vie Ouvrière, Bruxelles, 1983.

16. Abbreviation for *Geheime Staatspolizei* (secret state police), one of the two sectors of the German Nazi security police, which had its genesis in the SS (*Schutzstaffel*, defense echelon). *Petit Dictionnaire Larousse*, p. 1368. Librairie Larousse, Paris, 1971. The New Colombia Encyclopedia, p. 2466. Colombia University Press. New York and London, 1975.

17. Jews were dismissed from their professions in November 1940. *Registre des Juifs* was ordered in December 1940. In June 1942, Jews' assets were blocked and their businesses confiscated, and the compulsory wearing of the yellow star was implemented. Steinberg, Maxime, *La Question Juive 1940-1942*, pgs. 68, 77, 78, 112. Vie Ouvrière, Bruselles, 1983. Photocopies of the registry questionnaire filled out by my father, dated January 13, 1941, were furnished to me by the good auspices of the *Musée Juif de Belgique*. My father had registered all of us, i.e., himself, my mother, and all three of their children: my brother (who was no longer in Belgium), my sister, and myself.

18. Steinberg, Maxime 1942 *Les Cent Jours de la Déportation des Juifs de Belgique*, pgs. 143-152. Vie Ouvrière, Bruxelles, 1984.

19. *Memorial de la Deportation des Juifs de Belgique*, by Serge Klarsfeld and Maxime Steinberg. The Beate Klarsfeld Foundation, New York, N.Y., 1982. Ibid., pp. 327, 469. Steinberg, Maxime, 1942 Les *Cent Jours* . . ., p. 148.

20. Steinberg, Maxime, *La Question Juive 1940-1945*, pgs. 127, 142. *Les Cent Jours de la Déportation*, p. 34. The AJB (*Association des Juifs de Belgique*, Association of Jews of Belgium) "under the continual threat of the occupying forces, was operated for the cynical purpose of creating a body of Jewish spokespeople to serve as forced intermediaries in efficiently enforcing the application of anti-Jewish measures." Pro Museo Judaico V.Z.W., p. 11, *The Malines Museum of Deportation and Resistance,* Michel Laub C.C.I.B., Brussels, June 1995.

21. *Mémorial de la Deportation des Juifs de Belgique*, pgs. 20, 151, 155.

22. Ibid., pp. 26, 155, 315.

23. *Mémorial de la Déportation des Juifs de Belgique*, 1982, pgs. 30-31, 212.

24. While processing their captives in the antechamber of the Caserne Dossin, the Nazi bureaucrats robbed the Jews of their slightest valuable possessions, which they sold outside the assembly camp. Steinberg, Maxime, *La traque des Juifs 1942-1944*, Volume I, p. 217. Vie Ouvrière, Bruxelles, 1986.

25. This family was deported from Malines on August 25, 1942, in convoy V. Among the 995 deportees were 232 children. Upon arrival at Auschwitz on August 27, 1942, 780 people were gassed. *Mémorial de la Déportation des Juifs de Belgique*, pgs. 22-23, 477.

26. Steinberg, Maxime, *La Traque Traque des Juifs 1942-1944*, Volume I, p. 95, 1986.

27. Camille Adolph Gutt was born in Brussels, Belgium, on November 14, 1884. He was Belgian Finance Minister from 1934 to 1935, and from 1939 to 1945. He went into exile to Great Britain with the Belgian government when Germany invaded Belgium, and he remained in London during the German occupation. He returned home when Belgium was liberated. Although his parents had converted and he was a Protestant, "Gutt was repeatedly attacked in anti-Semitic statements by Belgian Fascists," *Current Biography, Who's News and Why*, p. 264, 1948. The H. W. Wilson Co., New York, N. Y., 1949, pgs. 263-266.

28. *Mémorial de la Déportation des Juifs de Belgique*, 1982, pgs. 30, 212.

29. *Université Libre de Bruxelles* protested against the anti-Jewish ordinances. It closed its doors on November 25, 1941, after an injunction by the German occupier nominated an activist of the First World War to the Chair of Flemish Literature. Steinberg, *La Question Juive*, p. 117, 1983.

30. Please see note 21.

31. *Mémorial de la Déportation des Juifs de Belgique*, 1982, pgs. 26, 315.

32. Please see note 18.

33. Please see note 19.

34. *Mémorial de la Déportation des Juifs de Belgique,* 1982, pgs. 28-29, 327.

35. Please see note 23.

36. The Fort of Breendonk dates back to the fifteenth century. It was used by the Belgian troops during the First World War. It was chosen as General Headquarters of the Belgian Army in 1940. On September 20, 1940, and throughout the occupation, the German Nazis transformed the fort into the only concentration camp on Belgian soil. *The Fort at Breendonk,* published by the Board of Directors of Fort Breendonk Memorial, pgs. 7, 13.

37. "Kaddish as a prayer for the dead . . . transforms the mourner's moan of personal grief into a chant of sanctification for the Creator." Nathan Ausubel, *The Book of Jewish Knowledge,* p. 237. Crown Publishing, Inc., New York, 1964.

38. This museum consists of a room of 300 square meters. *Musée Juif de Belgique, Bulletin trimestriel,* January 1993, p. 1. "The Flemish Community, Province of Antwerp and City of Malines wanted to devote a space in the 'Hof van Habsburg,' which is the new name for the Dossin barracks, to a museum, 'The Museum of Deportation and Resistance,' which will thus become one of the rare museums in Europe to bear witness to the tragedy suffered by the Jewish people during the Second World War and located in one of the places that itself served as an antechamber for the extermination of the Jewish people." *Pro Museo Judaico V.Z.W.,* p. 4., 1995. It was inaugurated on May 7, 1995, by Albert II, King of Belgium.

39. The organization named "ÖFF" for *Östereichige Freiheits Front,* (Austrian Freedom Front), was started in London by Austrian refugees who had fled the Nazis. These Austrians were registered under "non enemy Germans." The establishment of the ÖFF was instrumental in having this listing changed to "Austrians." After Liberation, the sister organization in Belgium was housed at no. 8, rue de Toulouse in

Brussels. The youth movement of the organization was named "FÖJ" for *Freie Östereichige Jugend* (Free Austrian Youth).

40. Please see note 18.

Bibliography

Caestecker, Frank, *Ongewenste Gasten, Joodse Vluchtelingen en migranten in de dertiger jaren*, VUBPRESS, Brussel, 1993; Vluchtelingen Beleid in de Naoorlogse Periode, Balans. VUBPRESS, Brussel, 1992.

Fabry, Joseph, *The Next-to-Final Solution, A Belgian Detention Camp for Hitler Refugees*, Peter Lang Publishing Inc., New York, 1991.

Fein, Helen, *Accounting for Genocide, National Responses and Jewish Victimization during the Holocaust*. Free Press, New York, 1979.

The Fort of Breendonk, Published by the Board of Directors of Fort Breendonk Memorial.

Garfinkels, Betty, *Belgique, terre d'accueil, Problème du Réfugié 1933-1940*. Edition Labor, Bruxelles, 1974.

Klarsfeld, Serge, and Steinberg, Maxime, *Mémorial de la Déportation des Juifs de Belgique*, The Beate Klarsfeld Foundation, New York, 1982.

The Malines Museum of Deportation and the Resistance, Pro Museo Judaico, V.Z.W. Michel Laub, Bussels, 1995.

Miller, Judith, *One, by One, by One*, Simon and Schuster, New York, 1990.

Papanek, Ernst, *Out of the Fire*. Morrow, New York, 1975.

Pauley, Bruce, F., "Austria" in *The World Reacts to the Holocaust*, Ed. Wyman, David, S. Johns Hopkins University Press, Baltimore and London, 1996.

Steinberg, Maxime, *L'Etoile et le Fusil, La Question Juive 1940-1942*, Vie Ouvrière, Bruxelles, 1983; *L'Etoile et le Fusil, 1942 Les Cent Jours de la Déportation des Juifs de Belgique*, Vie Ouvrière, Bruxelles, 1984; *L'Etoile et le Fusil, La Traque des Juifs 1942-1944*, Volume I, Vie *Ouvrière, Bruxelles, 1986; L'Etoile et le Fusil, La Traque des Juifs 1942-1944*, Volume II, Vie Ouvrière, Bruxelles, 1986.

Steiger, Sebastian, *Die Kinder von Schloss La Hille*, Volumes I and II. Brunnen-Verlag, Basel, 1992.

AFTERWORD

COMMENTARY BY CLAUDETTE BEIT-AHARON.

My mother's book is a gift for all our family so that we can remember and mourn the loss of all those people we never had the privilege to meet, and those we knew who suffered to the end of their days with the horror of what they lost.

My Grandmother Helene, I knew as a bitter, sad, and always profoundly disoriented person. She never mastered English enough to have a regular conversation with me. She had a beautiful singing voice, but always sang those same songs of her youth in Vienna, *Wien, Wien, nur Du allein*, and others, because for her, after she left Vienna, life would never be truly sweet again, though she was to live another forty-three years. She was, even as a very old lady, extremely pretty, and looked at least ten years younger than she was.

I remember her sitting in front of the TV with my Grandfather Saly, in the mid 60s. The strong, overwhelming Florida sun was streaming through the closed white drapes of the "Florida room" in Hollywood. They were watching a documentary about Hitler's triumphant entrance into Vienna, the crowds roaring their approval, the buildings strewn with banners. They sat through the whole program shaking their heads, saying "my, my," as if they still couldn't believe that it had really happened. I remember asking them why they were watching it, why torture themselves, they knew all that would be said, they had been there! But for some reason they were riveted by the show. Maybe they wanted to be sure that the story was told correctly, and that the Austrians weren't left off the hook. I implored them to turn it off, but they couldn't. They sat there mesmerized, with tears in their eyes.

My grandfather had a much better command of English, and I remember many nice conversations with him. He told me about waiting as a young man in Munich all night with his sister Frieda (also murdered with her husband after they were deported from Nice, France) to get tickets to hear the great Caruso. He was a wonderful grandfather and I loved him dearly. He died in 1975 while I was in Israel. He has visited me in my dreams, so vivid I can smell his scent, and see his tummy jiggle when he laughs. He told me how he felt about many things in life, when I was a teenager. One conversation stands out clearly in my mind. I was fourteen years old, and I was sitting with him in his little white Toyota - then, in the early seventies such small cars were a novelty. It was a balmy Florida evening, my parents, sister and grandmother had gone for a stroll. I elected to stay behind with him because his legs gave him trouble and he couldn't walk very far. We talked about his life long before the war, when he had a store in Munich. He told me about his sisters and other friends, bike trips with his brother-in-law Jacques, and other high jinks of his youth. He said it was sad for him that we didn't know German, since this English business was so hard for him and "Mama." He never referred to my grandmother by her first name. They always called each other "Mama" and "Papa."

Growing up I was always very aware of my mother's insecurities, and her ambivalence about her identity from so many directions, her attempts to appear all American, or in different circumstances she would be Belgian. I had always known her to wear her heart on her sleeve. Clearly she must have had some skills as a child in concealing her feelings, or she wouldn't have survived. I remember her being incredibly (to me, at the time) upset when I told her that what she thought of a person or situation was written all over her face, or that a friend found her accent charming. She strove to have no accent.

I always thought that given her background, she coped pretty well. But I understood that there were triggers to be avoided, and I avoided them. Somehow I knew that they were not about me at all, and the source was something that I couldn't understand. Her growth through writing these memoirs has been truly amazing. Though the journey was difficult and painful the results have been constructive. It is sad that my Grandparents couldn't live to be part of the healing — forty years was not enough time.

My grandparents never talked about their daughter Herta. I believe that they could no longer bring themselves to tell her story, it was too painful for them. They would just point out her picture and sigh. My grandmother especially was very untrusting of the intentions of the world at large. She had a hard time letting us out of her sight when we visited them in Florida. She had good reason to feel that way, and to be obsessed about abductions. We laughed off her seriousness at the threats that she perceived everywhere, which must have been especially frustrating for her.

Growing up, I knew somehow that my mother didn't feel that she had definite proof that her sister Herta had died. When I went to Israel in 1974 at eighteen, I felt that I should be looking for Herta. Perhaps she had survived. I searched the faces on the bus in Haifa, those broken people with the tattooed numbers on their arms, for traces of the pretty young woman whose face had always occupied a central spot in my grandparents' home. I tried to force myself to go to the *Yad Vashem* museum and try to look her name up - but somehow the thought was paralyzing. I dreamed of a reunion . . . My poor Grandpa died at about that time. But still I half looked for her in every public place.

I am never comfortable unless I have a valid passport, and I always know that it is close by.

I am fair skinned and have blue eyes. As a little girl I had blond hair. This pleased my Mother no end. She always admired northern European coloring, finding them more attractive than Jewish ones. I remember one day when I was thirteen, I came downstairs with my hair in two braids by my ears. She laughed and said "I could have named you "Gretchen." She was not indicating that this would have been a good idea, but was clearly pleased that I could have "passed" if I had to.

She had picked our names because of her love of French, but I think that our names were also part of her continuing hiding, and she just wanted us to be safe. But it was really ironic, for here I was, proud to identify as a Jew, and Jews were constantly questioning my origins because of a non-Jewish appearance, and my first name.

My mother, out of necessity, had hidden her identity, and one of the results was that she heard lots of anti-Semitic remarks that she might not have heard otherwise by so called friends. I was not interested in hiding at all, and yet I also heard many an anti-Semitic remark. Unless I made an announcement, bigots had no idea that one of "them" was hearing these statements. In order to protect myself from hearing these epithets, I always found a way to announce my ethnicity as soon as possible in social situations.

My Jewish identity and that of my children is supremely important to me. I pray and hope that they will sanctify the memories of our dear families, and all the extended family of the murdered Jewish People, by living strong lives of Jewish commitment. As I watched my mother's struggles with her insecurities, I decided that the only way that I could do something about what happened before I was born, was by living as positive a Jewish life as I could, and raise my children the same way.

Of course, none of this would have been possible if my mother had not been that defiant little girl in the convent school, resisting the brainwashing, brushing off the signs of the cross, and staying true to who she was.

In 1991, while I was a graduate student in New York City, by chance in an office some-where, I came across a glossy spread in New York Magazine describing the upcoming First International Gathering of Children Hidden During World War II. I had never truly understood my mother's reluctance to speak about, or really address her past, and I sent her that article, thinking that maybe this event might provide a new context for tracing that painful time.

As a child, I had always interpreted my mother's reluctance to speak of that time, and her apparent bitterness about it, as my being unworthy of hearing about such important things. Now, reading the book, I wonder if this feeling was passed on to me - the youngest in the family - in a way that mirrored how my mother was treated by the adults around her, during her own childhood. In order to protect her, they did not explain things to her, which left her feeling lonely, guilty, and confused. My mother, too, wanted to protect me. Unlike my sister, who says that she somehow always knew that my mother's feelings had nothing to do with her, I internalized or inherited a deep but vague sense of guilt, sure that I was to blame for my mother's bitterness, convinced that were I different, I could have prevented her feeling that way. Something was hidden - something very bad that we could never change.

This feeling in me began as guilt, and grew into anger and frustration during my adolescence, but with no way yet to pinpoint the roots of these feelings. Becoming an adult has for me, among other things, been a process of coming to understand the circumstances of my family history. Now, especially with the help of my mother's book, I begin to see that my mother's efforts to protect me from hurt she had suffered were, on one level, in vain; experience gets passed on if not directly, then indirectly. The chance to heal from the pain of that time, comes only with the direct confrontation with the past that this book offers.

Four years younger than my sister, as a child I knew my grandparents only as old people. I too was especially fond of my Grandpa and, like my sister, remember vividly how it felt to sit on his lap, his jokes, his little songs as he bounced me on his knee, "I love you, a bushel and a peck, a bushel and a peck, and a hug around the neck." Somehow, because of his accent, I thought of these as German or Yiddish songs, like "By mir bist du shein," when in reality these were all American ditties popular in the forties and fifties. But I did know my grandfather well enough that now, when I read about that terrible time when he said, sobbing: *"Mein bestest Kind haben sie mir genommen"* (They took my best child), I am transported to the moment and see and hear vividly, and feel deeply my little-girl mother's wretchedness.

Though I loved my grandmother, I found it difficult to understand her - literally, in terms of language, and more figuratively, in terms of her personality. Sometimes she frightened me with cruel jokes when I was very little. When I was a bit older, she would warn me not to go outside alone, saying "someone will shteal (steal) you . . . ." I scoffed at her idea, not knowing the roots of her fears. When she was very old, after my grandfather had died, she once warned me never to trust a non-Jew, because in reality they all want to kill us. Now that I understand, with the help of the details here, what my poor grandmother lived through, I know what she was trying to tell me, and that she wanted to protect me. With the help of my mother's book, I have come to know my grandparents better now, and to know my mother better too. I am also especially grateful to have a chance to know my aunt Herta a little bit. I was robbed of my aunt - and my uncle - and of the children they would have had, and I palpably feel that void.

When I was about eleven years old, I sang in a children's chorus the piece "I Never Saw Another Butterfly," based on poems by Jewish children who perished in the Nazi genocide. My grandparents attended a performance at our synagogue, and afterwards my mother told me that my grandfather had cried. Hearing this I felt at once guilty and confused. Was he just proud of me? But then, why would he cry? I could not understand the extent of his feelings and associations. I tried unsuccessfully to convince myself that this reaction was only sentimentality. But, with a lingering feeling of inauthenticity, I could sense that the truth must be too much for me to suddenly bear, that I was not fully enough a person to comprehend and participate in these feelings. I think now, though, that I was indeed enough of a person, and though it would have been hard, my mother and grandparents' confiding in me, would have grounded me in a way that I needed, as I moved into adolescence. But ultimately, there is no way to know in retrospect, what might have been best.

Certain bits of the story that my mother tells here, I have indeed known about since I was a child. For example, I knew that she would wipe off the sign of the cross when she was at the convent school, and the hiding among the furs when the Nazis came. But, never so vividly as told in the book. Or, the moment my uncle Ernst's girlfriend bought candies for my mother, the orange peels covered with chocolate. Other stories I had never heard; for example, that for quite some time my mother called herself "Irène." I do have a faint recollection, as a small child, of thinking that my aunt Herta was lost somewhere and might be found. Then, at some point, I sensed in my mother an unexplained shift to sadness and despair.

When I visited my parents soon after they returned from the meeting in Belgium (see Conclusion), my mother showed me the names of our murdered relatives listed in the *Mémorial de la Déportation des Juifs de Belgique*. Of course, I began to cry. My mother seemed surprised that I would cry, or maybe she was afraid that this could be so close to me, emotionally, after she had gone to such efforts to keep me at a distance from all this. But the message is clear, I appreciate her trying to protect me and my sister; who knows what other scars we would bear had she told us all when we were small.

Nevertheless, there was ultimately no way to avoid the pain, because it came through in other ways anyway. Also, not understanding my mother's feelings - for example, her relationship to the French language, and her wish that her daughters learn it impeccably - inevitably affected my growing up and formed my personality. In my life and work I champion the vernacular as a place of depth, resistance, difference, legitimacy, and I generally distrust official and chauvinistic cultures.

My identity as a Jew has long been important to me. My parents made every effort to provide me with a progressive Jewish education, and I was *Bat Mitzvah*. But, this particular history of my family has also always been with me, and this book validates us. It is our history, and it fills a hole or erases a question mark in my identity that was felt, but not fully understood.

In my teaching and research I fight against racial and ethnic bigotry, and toward cross-cultural understanding. Teaching in Virginia with relatively few Jewish students, I always note my background and my family history, and make analogies to the dangers of fascist ways of thinking and being. Race and ethnic hatred is still our biggest danger in this time, nationally and internationally. My own work, in Africa or in the United States, is integrated on all levels with my life and is deeply about combating hatred and fostering understanding.

The seeds of my life were sown, sometimes in mysterious ways, in the experience of my parents and grandparents. I thank my mother for the enormous effort it took to write this book, and I am deeply grateful to my father for loving and supporting my mother, to enable her to give us this very precious and lasting gift.

UNVEILED SHADOWS

THE WITNESS OF A CHILD

This very moving memoir eloquently represents the last voices to be heard from the holocaust. *Unveiled Shadows* is the relatively unheard testimony of those children who survived because they were hidden during the Nazi occupation of Europe. These terrified children saw loved ones taken away, and now, more than fifty years later, they give us the final documentation of their pain. As adults at the end of this century, the pain, the images, and the horror endure. Ingrid Kisliuk stands as a powerful voice for a generation whose childhood was stolen from them.

Sol Gittleman, Gantcher Professor of Jewish Studies,
Senior Vice President/Provost. Tufts University

Please send _____ copies of **UNVEILED SHADOWS.**
(ISBN: 0-9663440-0-6) @ $14.95 U. S. / $17.95 Canada.
Residents of Massachusetts please add $ 0.75 sales tax per book.

I am enclosing $ _____ , which includes $3.00 shipping and handling for the first book. For each additional book please add $1.00 for shipping. Send check or money order (no cash or C.O.D.s)

Name _____

Address _____

City/ State/Zip _____

 Please make checks payable to:
Nanomir Press
P. O. Box 600577
Newton, MA 02460
Fax: (617) 332-4770

Please allow 2 to 4 weeks for delivery.

UNVEILED SHADOWS

The Witness of a Child

This very moving memoir eloquently represents the last voices to be heard from the holocaust. *Unveiled Shadows* is the relatively unheard testimony of those children who survived because they were hidden during the Nazi occupation of Europe. These terrified children saw loved ones taken away, and now, more than fifty years later, they give us the final documentation of their pain. As adults at the end of this century, the pain, the images, and the horror endure. Ingrid Kisliuk stands as a powerful voice for a generation whose childhood was stolen from them.

> Sol Gittleman, Gantcher Professor of Jewish Studies,
> Senior Vice President/Provost. Tufts University

Please send _____ copies of **UNVEILED SHADOWS.**
(ISBN: 0-9663440-0-6) @ $14.95 U. S. / $17.95 Canada.
Residents of Massachusetts please add $ 0.75 sales tax per book.

I am enclosing $ _____ , which includes $3.00 shipping and handling for the first book. For each additional book please add $1.00 for shipping. Send check or money order (no cash or C.O.D.s)

Name _____

Address _____

City/ State/Zip _____

Please make checks payable to:
Nanomir Press
P. O. Box 600577
Newton, MA 02160-0005
Fax: (617) 332-4770

Please allow 2 to 4 weeks for delivery.